The Learning Years

David Glenister

Table of Contents

*"We trained hard, but it seemed that every time
we were beginning to form up into teams, we
would be reorganized."*

*"I was to learn later in life that we tend to meet
any new situation by reorganising,
and a wonderful method it can be for creating
the illusion of progress while producing
confusion, inefficiency, and demoralisation."*

Caius Petronius (AD66)

Dedication

To all my police family colleagues and friends who when called upon to undertake any task did so to the best of their ability.

About The Author

He joined the Metropolitan Police Force in 1976, where on completion of basic training, was posted as a uniform constable at to Tower Bridge Police Station on 'M' Division. This was followed by a spell on several squads. In 1987 he became a Detective and was promoted to the rank of Detective Sergeant on the Homicide Command before retiring in 2006.

During his time in the police, the author received 18 commendations and awards. Whilst in the police he qualified as a teacher.

Since retirement the author completed a BA in Education and Training as well as a Diploma in Occupational Safety and Health.

The author currently works as a Health and Safety professional and trainer

---oooOooo---

Preface

When I joined the Metropolitan Police Force in 1976, it did not occur to me that my journey would take me through the seamier sides of life, dealing with an assortment of crimes that crossed the legal spectrum'. Along the way, I would learn how to adapt to constantly changing situations. I was not alone in this - many thousands of officers have also been subject to these changes.

As far as change goes, it seems the modern police force is managed in pretty much the same way as the Roman legions of yesteryear, with perceptions of change being espoused louder than its actual benefits. It seems to me that Caius Petronius's quotation is as accurate now as when he made it all those years ago.

Change then was a constant factor that needed to be circumvented. For example, there were four areas within the Metropolitan Police when I joined. Subsequently, this was increased to eight and later reduced to just five.

In all honesty, I cannot say that all the changes have made any difference to the way I or the police service in general worked - although it certainly cost the taxpayer many thousands of pounds and along the way seemed to create jobs for senior police ranks. One need only look at the cost incurred when Sir Ian Blair, Commissioner of Police, decided to add the word 'Together' into the 'Working for a

Safer London' logo. That single word cost the taxpayer many thousands of pounds to implement.

Luckily for me, I was privileged and fortunate enough to have been accompanied during salient parts of my police journey through the maze of life by close colleagues, as well as members of the general public. In particular one group of unsung heroes to whom both the public and police service owe a huge debt of gratitude; they are the lay magistrates. Other than claiming expenses, lay magistrates are unpaid and fulfil their tasks as a civic duty. Not only do they sit in court and handle the cases brought before them but also make themselves available for out- of -hours' house calls, often during unsociable hours, where an officer would attend to swear an oath to obtain an urgent search warrant. Over the years, I made that call to numerous lay magistrates who, without fail, accommodated me every time.

During my journey, and here I make use of ~~Using~~ the SAS parlance, a number of my fellow journeymen sadly, for one reason or another, did not 'Beat the Clock.' By that I mean they never completed the full term of office through to retirement.

This was due to many reasons; some of whom were seduced by the dark side where–officers were subjected to either criminal proceedings found guilty and sentenced by a court, or subjected to internal disciplinary proceedings resulting in their dismissal or enforced resignation. Others sadly passed away whilst others were permitted to retire on the grounds of ill health, others left to pursue other careers.

This book is based on my recollection of events during the first six years of my police service, which may not be exactly as others recall them, and which I have recorded to the best of my ability.

This book by no means covers everything I did during this period, as to do so would require a much larger tome. It does though provide an overview of what life at the coal face was like.

Where people need to be protected or to avoid causing unnecessary upset, some names have been altered. Any mistakes that may have been made are mine and mine alone. My decision to write the account of my journey is to enshrine for posterity the events that took place during my police career so that I can, hopefully, bring to life some of the everyday occurrences that I encountered, along with that of my fellow police officers and to record it so that my memory can be refreshed when it begins to fade.

A special thank you goes to my wife Grace; my daughters Alex and Hannah, my good friend Clive, and all those who have had the misfortune to put up with the storytelling over and over again up to the point where they can now repeat them, word for word before I say anything!

---ooo0ooo---

Prelude to Application

The Great Train Robbery occurred in 1963, seven years before I left school to start work. Bruce Reynolds was the gang leader, which quickly became known in the media as 'The crime of the century.'

Bruce Reynolds has since talked about his involvement in the Great Train Robbery, alluding that information regarding the amount of money being carried that day by the mail train came from a crooked lawyer that he never named.

I could not imagine then that when I left school in 1970 with little in the way of qualifications that I would end up working for a solicitor's office that had represented Thomas Wisbey and two other members of the great train robbery; when they first appeared for trial at the Central Criminal Court Old Bailey.

As an outdoor clerk for a firm of solicitors based in the Strand London WC2, it was the first time I met Ellis Lincoln. I can still visualize him sitting at his big desk in his first-floor office overlooking the Strand, running the office as a conductor does with a band. Ellis had been a high-flying solicitor, but he was working in a legal executive-type capacity specializing in criminal court cases when I knew him.

Ellis Lincoln had a checkered career as a solicitor. For a time, he was publicly courted as the solicitor of choice for prominent criminals that included three of the Great Train Robbery members and Aloysius Lucky Gordon. Gordon was a society figure linked to Christine Keeler – the call girl at the centre of the Profumo scandal. It led to the resignation of John Profumo, the then Secretary of State for War, with considerable collateral damage that contributed to the Government being defeated at the 1964 general election

Ellis's fall from grace occurred in 1966 when following a Law Society disciplinary hearing, he was found guilty on two matters. One was for conduct, unbecoming a solicitor, and ~~secondly~~ the other for using the client's money for his own purposes. Using other people's money, was not a part of the role expected of solicitors. I do not know whether that money came from his Great Train Robbery clients, but it didn't matter either way as Ellis whilst no longer a solicitor was still working in a legal executive capacity dealing with criminal court cases.

My parents told me I could trust solicitors and people in authority, a belief that had well and truly been burst wide open and now lay in tatters on the floor. It was a salutary lesson to learn – trust no one.

My position as an outdoor clerk meant I was continuously attending Crown Courts and barrister's chambers where I would work alongside and on behalf of alleged criminals, most of whom were looking at ways to mitigate their crimes either to receive a reduced sentence or to use the system to return a not guilty verdict. Working with criminals did not sit right with me. I was thankfully well out of that profession, and apart from throwing stones at park keepers and scrumping for fruit in back gardens, I was pretty much a goody-two-shoes who had never been in trouble with the police.

Therefore, my current work was diametrically opposite to what my parents had taught me. Criminals I was told needed to be punished, and I saw myself working on behalf of society to do just that. Trusting no one was the key message I took from my time as an outdoor clerk – that and the desire to become a police officer.

The problem I now faced was how to go about doing that. Unfortunately, at my tender age of 17, with poor educational qualifications and a general lack of life experiences, I had to be patient and wait until the right opportunity came; when I could apply and hopefully pass an interview for the office of police constable with the Metropolitan Police. To gain that experience, I left Lloyd Raymond & Co for another outdoor clerk position before in turn becoming a clerical officer with the 'Action Department' of the Queen's Bench Division at the Royal Courts of Justice in the Strand

The term 'Action Department' was somewhat misleading as the work was mundane and repetitive. The positive was that you were required to interface with members of the public, which occasionally provided some light entertainment.

On one occasion, I was behind the counter when a man entered and passed over documentation for a writ of summons to take out legal proceedings against Her Majesty Queen Elizabeth II. He wanted to sue 'Mummy' for not recognizing him as her illegitimate son, thus denying him his right to be first in line to the throne. As the law stands, civil and criminal proceedings cannot be taken against the Queen, so 'her son,' a somewhat strange cookie, was politely sent on his way.

After more than two years with the Lord Chancellors Department, I decided in late 1975 that the time was right to make my application for the office of Police Constable in the Metropolitan Police Force (Now Police Service), which I duly completed and sent off for consideration.

I suspect that if I had applied now, in this current work climate, with the qualifications I had back then, I would not get through the initial paper sift process, let alone get through to an interview proper. Luckily, I had half a chance back then, and I was prepared to take it

---ooo0ooo---

Chapter 1

Application & Medical

Lo and behold, a few months later, just as I was giving up hope of hearing anything (yes, some things are still not rushed), I received a letter from the Metropolitan Police inviting me to attend an interview. The interview was a whole day affair taking in written exams, a medical and an interview. If you failed the exams or medical, you never got to the final interview and were sent on your way. Success in all three elements led to the offer of a probationary police officers position. The interview took place at **Paddington Police Station.**

I passed the literacy and numeracy tests and then progressed to the medical examination. The first thing that entailed was to remove all my clothes in preparation for a 'Full Monty' in front of a medical panel. To protect my modesty until that time, I was given a white robe without a wraparound belt that was about three sizes too big to wear. I had to hold it tight to prevent it from opening and giving a free thrill to the other interviewees and selection board personnel. Ironically, a bit like the continuous changes made by the police forces, my body had over time changed, meaning that the white robe would have fit me perfectly now. The medical process was well choreographed, and like automatons, we, the hopeful candidates followed each other about like lambs to the slaughter, moving along the row of chairs around the various examination stations. The medical was certainly in depth and included height and weight, lung capacity measurements, teeth & eyesight examinations, blood pressure, and a battery of questions on my parents and my own general health that I was required to answer. Towards the end of this medical examination process, I was called into a room and told to stand in front of three people sitting behind a desk. Following an initial introduction, the panel chairperson gave me directions on what to do. It went a bit like this…

'Stand in front of us and place your feet onto the painted marks on the floor facing this way.'

I looked down at the floor and saw four footprints painted on the floor. Two footprints faced towards the panel, and the other two, away from the panel. I did as I was told and placed my feet on the footprints facing the panel

'Take your robe off and drop it on the ground.'

I did that too – parading myself in front of them naked as the day I was born thinking to myself what next……

Let me tell you that standing naked in front of people is not something I would normally do, not even as a party piece, and to be honest, it felt a bit uncomfortable, to say the least. Especially, with three sets of eyes looking at me 'tackle out;', or so it seemed. After what seemed like an eternity, although in all probability it lasted only a few seconds or so, I was told to turn around and place my feet on the other two floor footprints facing the opposite way so that they were now looking at my back and buttocks. I turned around and placed my feet as directed, which is when one of the panelists said, '*Now bend over and touch your toes,*' which luckily I could do back then. Once that was achieved, the next command was '*and now you can spread your cheeks…*', so placing my hands on either side of my buttocks, I spread my cheeks. This set my mind racing as to what they were looking for or hoped to see …

It's funny, but when I feel uncomfortable, one of my coping strategies is to take my mind into another place and concentrate fully on that. On this occasion, I could see myself sitting in front of the television show 'Star Trek', which was all the rage. Every episode opened with the statement '*to boldly go where no man has been before seeking out new life forms.*' Well, if the panelists were secret Trekkie fans looking to go boldly, then they were looking in the wrong place to find Klingons or any other alien life form for that matter.

I held my position for them to have a good look, after which I was told to stand up put my gown back on, and with the medical now over, I left the room.

I do not know whether the sparkle from the family jewels or my impressive mooning skills made an impression. Still, I progressed on to the third and final hurdle – the formal interview, after which I was told then and there I had passed and would be sent a letter inviting me to join the Metropolitan Police Force as a probationary police officer.

Fast forward almost 40 years, and the application process is no longer that simple. Thank God I never had to jump through the hurdles faced by today's new police recruits, where they have to pass each stage before they are selected. Failure at any stage means you get shown the door, and that's it, pal; your off.

A friend of mine applied for a police constable position some time back. The selection procedure then required applicants to write a war and peace application form that had to pass muster, after which you would progress onto the next stage. That stage required you to sit three psychometric tests designed to hopefully separate the wheat from the chaff. Pass that, and you were asked to attend a 1-day practical assessment and interview. Pass that, and you were asked back for the 1-day physical test. Pass that, and to cap it off, you needed to spend £1000 or so to pass a Knowledge of Policing Certificate before being offered your position as a probationary constable.

Call me old-fashioned, but it seems a lot more complicated than it should be, although to be fair it does secure a number of civilian jobs needed to manage such a veritable marathon for applicants to pass. So much for change.

I doubt I could have been bothered to go through such a process, but luckily for me, I was spared, and so it was that Hendon Police College was my next stop.

---ooo0ooo---

Chapter 2

Hendon

On 18th October 1976, after packing a suitcase and bidding my parents farewell, I went to Paddington Police Station, where along with the other police recruits, I was ushered onto a coach and taken to the 5th-floor conference at New Scotland Yard to collectively swear the oath of constable in front of a senior police officer. Police officers are personally 'appointed' as such by the Crown. The oath taken reiterates an individual's allegiance to serve the Queen with fairness, integrity, diligence, and impartiality in the constable's office, particularly to preserve her peace. This was the starting date for once sworn in, my term as a probationary police officer commenced – a position I would retain for two years until confirmed in the rank.

From New Scotland Yard, we were taken straight to Hendon, where after a short briefing, we were shown around the Hendon College Estate, which was to be my home for the next 16 weeks. Strict male and female segregation applied with male recruits being shown through to their rooms in 'A' block and female recruits being shown through to their rooms in 'C' block. The blocks were out of bounds to each other and any infringements 'brought down the wrath of God' on the offenders – basically, you would be sent packing back to Civvie Street. Once we had deposited our personal belongings in our allocated accommodation, we returned to the recruit's canteen where we all met up again for a late lunch.

My course tutors Inspectors, Murray and Awty, were with us throughout, and after lunch, our photographs, fingerprints, and formal paperwork such as next of kin forms were processed.

The schedule for the next 16 weeks of training was explained. The course was split into three separate sections, two of five weeks and one of six weeks. Each section had an end-of-section exam that had to be passed in order for you to proceed onto the next section. So no pressure there then, the message was crystal clear - fail, and you are out.

After a good night's sleep, we were issued with clothing and our appointments the next day. Appointments included a whistle and key on a chain, a brown leather wallet, and a plastic notebook holder complete with a form 29. Male officers were also issued with a wooden truncheon. With regards to our appointments, we were required to carry these at all times, and on request, they had to be produced and shown to the tutors. Failure to produce the appointment when requested was punishable with an evening re-parade in front of the on-call duty officer.

What you may ask is the relevance of form 29. It was a relic from a by gone time, when the horse was one of the main means of travel. Someone had developed the form 29 for use in dealing with an injured horse. The form basically allowed me to authorise an attending vet to destroy and dispose of a horse should it be necessary. Now, why in the modern age of the motorcar was this still being issued.

Well, obviously, we did because this form gave rise to a lesson in itself. Important information was passed during this session, with the tutor providing some exciting snippets such as…..

Did we know that a bolting horse was extremely dangerous? – Fascinating, thanks for that - I never thought that a ¾ ton bolting animal was dangerous.

Did we know how to stop a runaway horse? – The secret was to run in the same direction as the horse, grab the halter and slowly bring it to a stop – clearly cutting edge information.

Now, although I considered myself reasonably fit and thanks to the physical training I would be getting through, my fitness levels would increase, but it would still have to be a very slow horse, one ready for the knacker's yard, for me to have any hope of matching it stride for stride and somehow catch it. In fact, to put it mildly, there was not a snowball chance in hell that I would be stupid enough to even attempt to stop a running horse.

I decided straight away this was not something I was going to worry about, and I was proved right as, during the whole of my 30 years of service, I never saw an upset or collapsed horse, let alone have to deal with a runaway horse, not even a police horse.

The third day was when the real work began to mentally and physically prepare us for what lay ahead. The gloves were well and truly off – for them to have meaning, practicals had to be as real as possible to prepare us to deal with the everyday situations we would meet in the real world. It would take several pages just to bullet point the list of everyday situations we might encounter. Still, the blended mixture of classroom-based theory interspersed with practical-based role play would see us alright – at least that's what our tutors said. The role plays covered many scenarios of dealing with people incidents, accidents, traffic processes, and arrests.

During this first week, the police stores issued each recruit with virtually every clothing and equipment required to kit out a police officer in the field other than everyday boots that the recruit had to provide. Why that should be, I don't know.

Sid Butcher was a name that conjured up fear in probationers. Sid was the drill sergeant who would scream and shout at recruits from morning through to night and an acknowledged expert on boots. At least that's what we thought at the time. I needed boots, but Hendon College was a good walk away from the local shops, so the problem presenting itself early on was where on earth I was going to get boots from. Sid arranged that one out for all of us, recommending the on-site shop as the place to go to. And that was exactly where I went to and bought my first and only pair of leather-soled boots. I buffed them up as much as I could, but they were never as shiny as the ones Sid wore.

I have reflected on my days at Hendon and spoken to a few colleagues who went through Hendon during Sid's reign. Without fail, all were given the same recommendation on buying boots, and funnily enough, he took over the shop's franchise when he retired. Who knows, maybe he had a vested interest or shares in the place. As for his recommendation to buy leather-soled boots, it may sound great, but on leaving training school, I learned their limitations to my cost. Those limitations were exposed on my first week out of training school when I was working night duty at Tower Bridge. I was the front seat passenger in a panda being driven by an old sweat sergeant when we chased a stolen vehicle. The driver abandoned the car in Catlin Street and ran into the Bonamy Estate, with me in pursuit. I was unfamiliar with the area, although soon found out that the Bonamy Estate was a rabbit warren, with slippery surfaces everywhere not conducive to the grip provided by my leather-soled boots. The person I was chasing wore training shoes and seamlessly twisted and turned through the walkways without missing a beat whilst I was sliding past turns, gradually getting further and further behind, until I turned a corner to find the driver was nowhere to be seen. I was really annoyed about that and resolved there and then that when I could afford a decent pair of boots, my leather-soled boots were going to be consigned to the rubbish bin.

The theory training at Hendon covered topics that included theft, assaults, road traffic, and drugs, with paragraphs having to be learnt word perfect. This learning was continually reinforced by tutors who would suddenly ask round-robin questions during classroom and practical role-play sessions. Learning topics word perfect was a necessary evil that instilled in recruits the knowledge needed to achieve a pass mark for the course exams. It was not for the faint-hearted as failure at any point to achieve the pass mark would lead to them being back classed with dismissal from the course following a second failure.

Tutors pushed the boundaries of decency in their efforts to develop confidence in individuals that would enable them to deal in any given situation. It was common for course tutors to embellish practical scenarios to cause maximum embarrassment to the role player. Although it seemed harsh at the time, the end result justified the embellishment. One scenario I recall involved a woman officer reporting an injury in the home. It went like this

‚Recruit 'Tell me what exactly your injuries are, please?'

Tutor 'I've injured my back.'

Recruit 'How did you injure your back?'

Tutor 'Well, it's like this. I was making love to my girlfriend; you know, kissing her on the lips gave her a good seeing to. It was in the throes of passion that the ceiling light fitment fell straight onto the small of my back.

Recruit 'That's an unlucky thing to happen.'

Tutor' Unlucky, I'm the luckiest man around.'

Recruit 'Why is that then?'

Tutor 'Cos 5 seconds earlier, and it would have fallen onto my neck and killed me – know what I mean', giving her a knowing wink in the process.

The woman officer went bright red, and although sharing her embarrassment, we all laughed. The point of the exercise had been made - never prejudge a situation and always expect the unexpected

On another occasion, an instructor, the class had not seen before came into the classroom. We were not told what this lesson was about – we were soon to find out.

The first words spoken were in a loud and aggressive manner. 'You are a shower - Sit up straight. This isn't kindergarten, you know. Call yourselves police officers – don't make me laugh', and with that, as an introduction, he turned his back on us, switched on an overhead slide projector that threw a white light onto the whiteboard, and then spent a while selecting a sheet to place on the projector. While he was doing this, a whispered comment was made by one of the recruits that elicited a 'who said that' from the instructor. The person responsible held his hand up and identified himself, after which the instructor said,' tell me what you just said?'

The culprit answered, 'I just said it looked like a white cat on a snow background.'

Instructor - 'Really, and you think that's funny. I don't - get out and go to the commandant's office. You are no longer a police recruit. Goodbye.'

As our colleague was leaving the room, he continued, 'The rest of you listen up; mess with me, and you are out. Do we understand each other?' You could have heard a pin drop as we all nodded in unison whilst watching our former colleague leave the room. It was not a good place to be at that time.

With that, the Instructor continued pointing his finger at me and saying, 'List one of the statutory defences to assault.'

Luckily I was the first, so I answered 'by consent – a person can consent to common assault' I was out of the fire, but the next candidate came into his sights. Once he answered, it went to the next person and so on until someone couldn't think of an answer. Gotcha – the instructor's next victim had been chosen. Straight away, the instructor went to town. 'You are not very bright, are you? Do you think you are good enough to be a police officer? I don't – you can join your friend outside the commandant's office. For you also, the journey stops here. Go on go.'

As the second recruit stood up and started to cross the floor to leave the room, the classroom door opened, and our course tutors entered together with the recruit who had been sent away earlier. They were all smiling as they thanked our unknown instructor for his input; he also smiled and left the classroom. The first act was to send the two victims back to their seats to sit down, then after a short time to reflect, one of the tutors said, 'Did you like the way you were treated just then?' The answer was a resounding 'No' – absolutely not. The tutors went on, 'You will all shortly be in a position of authority. Remember, it's very easy to abuse that authority. You didn't like the way you were treated just a moment ago, so don't abuse that power with others'

Lesson learnt – treat people with respect and be courteous at all times. In short, treat people as you would like to be treated.

---ooo0ooo---

Chapter 3

It's a MAD, MAD, World – check location

The world in 1976 was still coming to terms with the possibility of global Armageddon, where Mutually Assured Destruction (MAD) was still a distinct possibility. To prepare us for our role in the event of a pre-emptive nuclear strike, police recruits were given civil defence training. After my in-depth 1-day course, I would be a fully trained civil defence member – really. Unless they are holding back on something, I-didn't think that would be the case. Either way, our two instructors, who we affectionately named 'Neutron Ned' and 'Roentgen Ron', were full of it. These two were supercharged, almost nuclear powered as they rattled through the various types of radiation we were likely to be exposed to, even demonstrating how we would use a Geiger counter and a personal dosimeter to determine our dosage individual exposure levels. Telling whether someone had had too much radiation in one go was easy – They were either dead or had been vaporized into the atmosphere leaving a few ashes to remember them by.

The cunning plan had been put together by some Government spook who would of course be safe within his secure Kelvedon Hatch type underground nuclear bunker was simplicity itself. In the prelude to a nuclear strike, all police officers would be issued with their very own personal issue radioactivity dosimeter. A dosimeter worked on batteries and was about the size of a tipped cigarette. We would be carrying these dosimeters with us as tensions rose. When the four-minute warning went off, all the police officers on duty would run around their beats, blowing their whistles and telling everyone who would listen not to panic. With only a maximum of 4 minutes left to live they had to paint all their windows white to reflect the atomic bombs flash, whilst at the same time they had to run a bathtub full of water that was to sustain them within a safe haven until the radiation levels returned to a level that was safe.

This instruction was probably written by the same person who wrote about stopping a galloping horse. I imagined this picture of me running around like a headless chicken, a bit like Corporal Jones in Dad's Army shouting, 'Don't panic, don't panic.'

So during the last 4 minutes of my life, the Government wanted me to run around warning people not to panic before I along with them was to be vaporized and made part of the radioactive cloud that would circumnavigate the world a few times before returning to earth in another country. Who knows, instead of British, I could come back as a Russian – sort of swap sides, so to speak. Clearly, there was a serious flaw in what the Government expected me to do – the flaw being that I was not going to do it, and I suspect that neither were any of my colleagues. My preferred option in the event of a nuclear strike was to grab hold of a good-looking woman and head straight for the basement of the nearest pub, where we would hopefully spend the last few moments of our lives enjoying ourselves and collectively drinking ourselves into oblivion. Quite probably, I would be joined by my colleagues, so I guess the basement would have been quite snug, to say the least.

Luckily for everybody and especially the people of Rotherhithe and Southwark in particular, I was not called upon to test my highly tuned civil-defence skills.

---ooo0ooo---

Tower Bridge – Initial Posting

1977 - 1979

Chapter 4

Tower Bridge

On completion of my initial training at Hendon, I was posted to the 'M' Division who had responsibility for policing the London Borough of Southwark. The divisional H.Q. was based at Southwark Police Station. From there, the Commander held sway over the other six stations that made up the 'M' Division area – namely Camberwell, East Dulwich, Peckham Rotherhithe, Tower Bridge, and Carter Street (which later moved location and is now known as Walworth).

I was destined to become PC 293 MT; although it meant nothing to me as to where was I going to be based. The MT should have been a clue as it signified I was going to Mike Tango or in everyday police talk Tower Bridge Police Station. With its proximity to the docks, 'M' Division had in the past been considered a punishment posting for wayward police officers meaning they had to deal with drunken sailors, some of whom were from the punch first ask questions later school of dispute resolution. Thankfully the Pool of London and its docks had long ceased to be the Mecca of merchant ships, so in 1977 it was a lot quieter than it had been.

Leaving Hendon fully loaded down with plastic bags containing uniform and other goodies, the first stop was at Southwark Police Station, where I experienced at first hand the first crime of my career. Boy did they have a slick operation going. In no time at all; I was fleeced of the money I had not yet earned literally forced into signing a number of standing orders and direct debits that would pay monthly subscriptions to the likes of the Widow and Orphans fund, The Metropolitan Police Sports Fund, The Police Federation, The Federation Legal Insurance, The Group Insurance Scheme and the 4 Area lottery.

It was at Southwark that I first met PC 740 MT Steve Brown. Steve had passed out two weeks before me, but unfortunately for him, he had been selected to stay behind at Hendon College for a two-week stint providing site security.

There we were blissfully unaware that we were being posted to the same relief at Tower Bridge and would soon become good friends. With the documentation now complete, Southwark Police Station (otherwise known as Mike Delta) was left behind. A van arrived to take the two of us over to Tower Bridge police station (known as Mike Tango) to meet the station Superintendent.

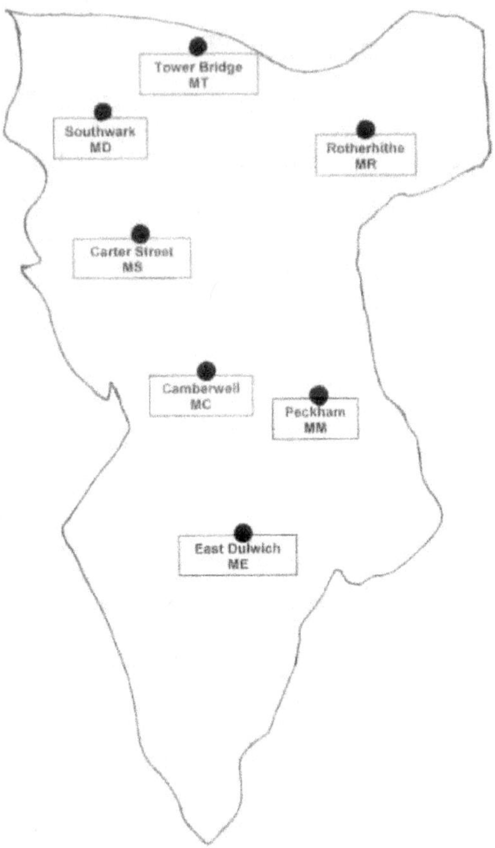

The Superintendent's office was on the second floor next to the canteen. Climbing the stairs to his office, we arrived and were told to wait in the canteen until summoned. Not needing to be told twice, that's exactly what we did. We went straight into the canteen and found an empty table where we both sat down. We had been sitting there for about 5 minutes when an old sweat P.C. came up to us and said, 'You are sitting at our table – Move. You can sit over there, and with that, he indicated at a table and chair in a far corner. Not the friendliest of greetings, but despite being a bit narked, it was our first day, and not wanting to create an issue we did as instructed.

Sod's law was that without knowing it, we had broken a station taboo by sitting uninvited at a table used by the card school. Serious stuff indeed. That was punishable by immediate ex-communication with a distinct possibility of becoming a social pariah – how unlucky was that. It seemed we had missed the lecture on the social pecking order of where to sit in police canteens. We learnt soon enough that it would take months before either of us were considered suitable candidates for elevation to the card school table membership, which was strictly limited to a formal invitation from all the members.

I had not been in my new seat long before I was summoned into the Superintendent's office. After the usual welcome speech, traffic process was brought up. Maybe he was an ex-traffic officer with a penchant for harassing drivers. Still, clearly, the traffic process was the order of the day as the Superintendent said, 'I expect you to complete process books on a daily basis.'

To this day, I am not certain why but, for some reason, the talk turned to traffic lights and, in particular, orange traffic lights, which he insisted meant the traffic had to 'Stop'. He instructed me to report all drivers who failed to stop at orange traffic lights for the offense of failing to comply with a traffic signal.

As a newly unwrapped knight with a duty to serve the public at large, I found this incongruous with the knowledge gained at Hendon that was still rattling around in my brains. So, instead of saying 'Yes sir, No sir, three bags full sir and so on, I didn't.

After all, was said and done, it was my duty to challenge inaccurate statements, so I replied,

'I don't think that's correct, sir. Orange means stop if it is safe to do so. It does not mean an offense has been committed unless the driver could have stopped but didn't.' The look on his face said it all really, and that's when the meeting went downhill.

The Superintendent said, 'I'm telling you orange means stop,' to which sticking to my guns I replied, 'I don't think that's right.'

Clearly, I was not supposed to disagree with the Superintendent, who replied, 'Interesting – I don't see you lasting long. Good day,' and with that, I was summarily dismissed.

It's strange, but I had that same argument with a police constable some 32 years later. I had been out of the police for a couple of years when whilst driving my car on a wet surface the lights changed from green to amber, I drove through them.

A short distance further on, I was stopped by a police officer who said, 'I have stopped you for driving through a red light,' I replied, 'It wasn't red, it was amber,' to which the policemen replied 'Amber means stop.' Talk about déjàvu. With that, I said, 'So we agree it was amber, you say I should have stopped, and I say it was safer to continue.' Despite being given a ticket, I am glad to say I was proved right on that occasion - but that's another story.

The Metropolitan Police operate 24 hours a day every day of the year. To do that requires officers working a relief system. At Tower Bridge, it was a 4 relief system with each shift lasting 8 hours. Parade times were 6 am (early turn), 2 pm (late turn), and 10 pm (night duty), with the fourth relief off on rest day.

To maintain cover during relief change, the wireless cars reported for duty an hour later than the rest of the relief. This differs from the current system which operates on a five-relief basis.

It just so happened that my relief had just finished early turn and had now gone home. I was told to report for early turn the next day, and that ended my first day as a police officer. The station van took me and my possessions to my new abode in room 66 at Maurice Drummond Section House

(The Drum), where I summarily dumped my belongings and went for a drink in the 'Mucky Duck' a local pub.

25

---ooo0ooo---

Chapter 5

Fresh as a Daisy

The next day, I got dressed in my uniform; and left my lodgings at the crack of dawn. Walking to the nearest bus stop, carrying a large clear plastic bag of Metropolitan Police goodies, I caught the very first bus that took me in the general direction of Tower Bridge Police Station.

As I got on the bus, it felt like all the passenger's eyes were burning into me as I took my seat on the lower deck. It's a strange feeling being the centre of attention, and when the bus conductress came up to me and made me aware that I might be required to deal with a passenger who had not paid the correct fare, I fairly went into a controlled panic. I still gave her the 'No problem, let me know' answer, but deep down, my mind was racing at 100 miles an hour trying to think back to the relevant scenario we had practiced at Hendon on what to do in such a situation; especially when it could quite possibly become the real thing. My first contact with the public and no communication or backup to rely on. Luckily for me, the passenger coughed up the rest of the fare, and my heartbeat returned to normal. The only visible signs of my angst were the beads of sweat running from my helmet into my eyes.

As soon as I could, I got off the bus on Jamaica Road, and like Santa Claus with his sack of goodies, I walked towards the police station to meet my fellow officers parading for an early turn.

There was an unwritten rule that reliefs would parade 15 minutes before the shift started to cover the previous relief as they left for home. No one questioned or complained why they were expected to work voluntary unpaid overtime – it was just the accepted norm. Whilst my relief was being paraded, I appeared at Tower Bridge police station or in the police phonetic code 'Mike Tango,' where I entered the front door and went up to the front office desk.

The station officer Peter was in the front office seated behind a desk with his head supported in his hands. As I entered, Peter blearily looked up from the desk in my direction and, upon seeing me, uttered the words 'Who the f*** are you? No, don't tell me, you're the new boy – you look fresh as a f***ing Daisy.' That's when Peter told me that I was a bit early as I wasn't expected to arrive at the station until 9 am. Either way, I had arrived.

I was admitted through to the station office and thence into the collator's office where I met the rest of my fellow 'A' relief colleagues who were introduced as Inspector Mc, Botty, J.T., Hips, Vulch, Blind Pugh, Beardy, Perce, Swold, and of course Pisspot the police cadet.

No one apart from Peter had a forename. In those days, individual nicknames were synonymous when working together in a close team, and it followed then that us newbies, Steve Brown and I, would be allocated a team nickname. My nickname was 'Daisy' because of the remark made on my arrival at the station that I was as 'fresh as a daisy.' I was known by that nickname from that date, and it followed me through my squad and station postings for the full 30 years –all thanks to a one-off comment made by Peter when we first met. As for Steve, his nickname came to be 'Ghurkha,' for no other reason than that, he had arrested no prisoners for a month, and as the saying goes, 'Ghurkha's don't take prisoners.'

In hindsight, I think we got off pretty light as other police officer nicknames included Mushy Peas, L.B.C., Beaker, Fruit bat, Bionic, Rubber bum, Bam Bam, Keyhole Kate, Chicken George, Zoom, Sinex, Wally, Mekon, Plug, Shaky and a few that are best left unsaid.

In common with other stations, Tower Bridge operated a four-relief system that provided a continuous 24-hour police response capability. Each relief was known simply as either A, B, C, or D, and they all used nicknames of some sort or another. Newbies were sent out from Hendon fully kitted out and I could feel the envious eyes of my fellow relief officers checking out the goodies all clearly on display in my clear plastic bag. Their eyes were like magnets, mentally noting everything. Clearly, looking to relieve me of some of the items, so I kept it pretty much attached to me for the first few hours of the day until I could acquire a secure locker to store my spare uniform and other goodies in securely.

My initial thoughts about my colleagues' intentions were confirmed as I went to find the station stores officer for a locker. He told me that police officers are all opportunists who would take someone else's kit if given the opportunity, and that would be the last you saw of it.

I was a fast learner, and it just so happened that an opportunity arose shortly after I met with the store's officer, whereby I acquired someone else's open locker. I removed their bits from it, and moved the locker to another location, where after stashing my stuff, I secured it with a locking padlock and stuck my name on it. As the saying goes, possession is nine points of the law.

Once my uniform and other items were safely stowed, I was taken around the station to meet some of the old sweat nine to fivers such as the beat crimes officer and plan drawer. I was also told about Mrs Smith, Liz, to her friends, who was the redoubtable night duty station telephonist and a veritable station legend. I would make her acquaintance in a week or so when my relief went onto night duty.

My first full day on relief finished at 2 pm, and luckily I got a lift back with J.T., who, like me, lived at the 'Drum'. It was J.T. who kindly provided me with a lift to and from Tower Bridge until I could afford a car of my own.

---ooo0ooo---

Chapter 6

Suffering with the D.I.A.

Luckily I joined the police in the age of new technology. The old system of having police telephone boxes strategically placed around the ground to phone into the police station had been superseded with a personal radio built of sheet metal that was extremely weighty and prone to poor reception. I think examples of this cutting-edge technology are now on show at the Science Museum.

Personal radios meant that you no longer had to look in the direction of the nearest police officer and blow your whistle to summon assistance; you could liaise directly with the station – assuming you had a signal; otherwise, you would pretty much be on your own.

After being trained with this high-tech equipment – it took at least a minute or two. I was released onto the streets of Bermondsey and Rotherhithe. The first two or three weeks, I was posted with seasoned officers on either foot or mobile patrol. During that time, I learnt about the local area, particularly the road names and beat boundaries. During this easing in period, I was involved in my first vehicle chase with a lost or stolen motor vehicle, which ended in a vicinity only accident. The accident involved a barrier gate leading into the Bonamy Estate, where the driver decamped from the vehicle and into its rabbit warren of paths and alleys. I got out and chased the driver, who clearly had two great advantages over me. The first was that he knew where he was going, and the second was he was wearing training shoes whilst I was wearing leather-soled boots. With nil traction on the boots, it seemed I lost distance on my prey at every turn leading to the inevitable, so when I turned the eighth or ninth corner, he was nowhere to be seen and was now lost in the estate. Not a particularly auspicious start.

Chastened, I put his escape firmly down to my basic lack of local knowledge and, to Sid Butcher, for some poor shoe advice. I needed to put this right, so I boned up on the names of roads and the various estates, and more importantly, I decided to buy a new pair of non-slippery boots when I could afford to do so.

On the flip side, I now knew that running in full uniform made you hot and sweaty. Lost in the estate, I was pretty despondent as I somehow found my way back to the scene of the accident, and that was when my first attack of the D.I.A.'s occurred.

Keeping fit at Hendon, running around in sports gear is one thing. Still, it's not until you actually use the uniform in real-life situations that you begin to identify problems with the issued clothing. It may be tough and hardwearing, but it was not as good as it was cracked up to be. In this instance, the offending items were the blue nylon shirt and the nylon trousers. The 'Dreaded Itchy Arse', otherwise known as the D.I.A.'s, was something most police officers experienced. It was an affliction that was prone to strike when you were involved in an energetic activity without any notice and usually when you were in close proximity to actually dealing with members of the public.

The D.I.A. attack was caused by dripping body sweat that travelled down the body, collected at the waistband of the trousers where it slowly seeped through into your pants, collecting in the cheeks of your bottom and genital area, causing an itch that immediately needed to be scratched. Basically, because nylon shirts and trousers don't breathe, body sweat never evaporates, hence the sweat droplets and damp pants.

As there was no knowing when this phenomenon would occur, the skill was needed to deal with it discreetly, so it did not draw unwanted attention. The solution was to find the corner of a nearby wall and then proceed to slowly gyrate your bottom from side to side as well as up and down, a bit like the scene from the 'Jungle Book' where Baloo scratches his back on a tree to remove an itch.

The wall stance was retained until the D.I.A. had passed, and you were able to resume your patrol, at least until the next attack, when the whole process was repeated.

Dealing with an attack of the D.I.A.'s was why so many police officers stood with their backs against a wall – it was not to feel safe – it was to deal with a D.I.A. attack.

I hear a lot about sexy nylon lingerie being worn in bed to spice up an intimate relationship. Still, from my experiences of D.I.A.'s, I don't believe body heat and nylon make particularly good bedfellows.

I suspect that this D.I.A. problem led to changes in police shirts – certainly during my time in uniform, the blue nylon shirts were replaced with white short-sleeved breathable cotton shirts – problem half solved.

---ooo0ooo---

Chapter 7

Drunk or not drunk

At the Hendon College passing out parade, I was presented with my 'black rover' warrant card. (This warrant card has now been replaced with a printed card bearing your picture and personal details). The issue of a warrant card was a passage of rite whereby all newly fledged police constables, for reasons best known to the courts, suddenly became expert police witnesses overnight on whether a person was drunk or not.

The telltale signs for a person being drunk were that they smelt of intoxicating liquor, were unsteady on their feet and had slurred speech for which a person could be arrested for being 'Drunk and Incapable'. As an expert witness, I could now give an opinion in a court of law that a person was 'Drunk'.

My second week at Tower Bridge saw me working night duty. It was during this time that the station reserve Botty called me up on the radio '293 from Mike Tango receiving.'

'Mike Tango from 293 – go ahead.'

'293 – there is a report of a drunk in Fendall Street near the junction with Grange Road. Go and check it out.'

'Mike Tango from 293 – en route.'

I went hotfoot to the location given, and sure enough, there was a male staggering all over the place, with slurred speech and smelling of intoxicating liquor. In my view, he was drunk and incapable, so I arrested him.

'Mike Tango from 293 - send the station van to Fendall Street to convey a prisoner to the station.'

'293 from Mike Tango – Mike Tango 2 (The station van) is en route.'

Placing him in the station van, we went to Tower Bridge Police Station. It was during that journey that my prisoner complained about his leg hurting. No reason was given as to the cause of the supposed leg injury. We went to the charge room, where I gave my evidence of arrest to the charge room sergeant. The prisoner's details were noted; he was charged and placed in a cell to appear the next day before the magistrates sitting at Tower Bridge Magistrates Court. Whilst in the cell that he continued to moan about a pain in his leg.

Luckily for him, Mushy Peas took over from the charge room sergeant when he went to lunch, and as the prisoner was still moaning, he decided to err on the side of caution and called out the divisional surgeon to attend and conduct an examination. Sure enough, the divisional surgeon arrived, but his initial examination found nothing untoward. As the prisoner was still complaining, he suggested the prisoner be taken to Guys Hospital for an X-Ray. A simple arrest had just gotten more complicated, for it meant he had to be taken under guard to the hospital, and as the arresting officer, that meant it would be me.

So off to the hospital with my prisoner, we went where an X-Ray was taken that identified a broken femur. My prisoner was immediately taken into the hospital as a patient and hospitalised for a few weeks.

It was no surprise that being the kind-hearted organisation the public expected the Police Force to be, we never continued with the offence of being 'Drunk & Incapable'.

I still added it as an arrest in my probationer event book to show my supervisors what work I had returned. Nothing else was heard from my prisoner, who I assume went on and made a full recovery.

I do not know how he broke his femur but I can say without a doubt, the police did not cause it. I suspect that were that same event to happen today, it would be a major enquiry where I would be served with a police complaint form 163 and investigated by a team of officers to find out the why's and wherefores of how his injuries occurred. The end result would have been a considerable cost to the public finances and still none the wiser as to how the injury occurred.

It just shows that even expert witnesses can sometimes get it wrong.

Chapter 8

Dropping in the smelly stuff

I had been at the Tower about a month when the relief was called into the station early to support the night duty relief on a particular operation. Acting Chief Inspector Sam Mac briefed us in the station canteen on a planned search of an illegal club operating from a house in Grange Road. There were even traffic officers present whose sole role was to enter the premises after it had been secured and light the inside of the house up with special 'Dragon lights'. I soon discovered that so-called 'Dragon lights' burnt extremely bright but used up enormous amounts of energy and gave off an incredible amount of heat in the process. They were superb whilst the charge lasted, but when it ceased, it did so immediately and without warning as Tommy Cooper would say 'just like that' leaving you with no night sight and in total darkness.

The information was that a squatted house was being used as an illegal club selling alcohol and drugs. Nowadays, this would be called a 'Rave'.

This particular night, a Friday, was expected to be very busy. It was explained that the house fronted onto Grange Road, although there was a rear yard that could be accessed from a side entrance exiting into Crimscott Street. The address was currently being watched by police officers from a fixed observation point.

Current information was, it was getting very busy, with access being solely through the front door. Sam Mac planned to have two attack teams. On the attack command, attack team 1 was to go straight through the front door whilst attack team 2 was to leave earlier, gain entry to the yard at the rear of the premises and when the attack command was given, was to enter the premises simultaneously from the rear.

I was in attack team 2. As a fit young probationer, my role was to climb over the external wall, descend into the rear yard area, and open the side gate in Crimscott Street through which the rest of my attack team was to enter discreetly; where we would wait patiently until the 'attack, attack' command was given.

Once inside the premises, my role would revert to that of exhibits officer – meaning I recorded and preserved evidential articles seized at the scene, through to taking them back to the station where they would be sealed and securely stored until needed at a court case. I'd like to think I had been specially selected for this role, but in reality, it was because no one else wanted to do it.

The attack was planned for around 1 am on a Saturday morning, so we ate early and prepared to take off. It was a very dark night when attack team 2 silently entered Crimscott Street.

Getting on top of the surrounding external wall was a piece of cake, even in my leather-soled boots. Getting down the other side was a problem as it was particularly dark with virtually no visibility into the yard's interior. So, getting down safely was a bit of a nightmare.

I slowly lowered my body down the wall feeling the way with my feet as I did so, dropping the last foot onto the backyard cobblestoned floor. That's when I heard the squish as my boots displaced something loose on the floor that squirted out to the sides. I immediately sensed something was not quite right, especially as my feet started slipping and sliding all over the place, followed by a horrible smell that assailed my nostrils. It was a close call but luckily, thank God I never fell head over heels because had I done so, I would have been covered in man poo - Yes, I was standing in the middle of literally hundreds of curly whirly human turds.

I thought of my father's advice when I joined the police 'David, whatever you do in the police, make certain you never drop in the poo' - maybe not using the word poo. Well, dad, have I got news for you…'Richard the thirds' were everywhere, and I mean everywhere. There were buckets of overflowing poo strategically interspersed around the yard, competing with groups of single deckers for floor space.

This was not a pretty sight, and the pervading smell was indescribably rank.

It was no wonder then that no-one used the yard door to enter and leave, as to do so invited untold dangers, with the absolute certainty of leaving with poo covered shoes.

I located the yard door and released the bolts, which allowed me to pull the door inwards. In doing this, I pushed a shedload of dried Richards into a pile by the wall, an action that removed the Richards hardened top surface, releasing even more of an odious smell. Up to this stage, the rest of my attack team were blissfully unaware of what was in store for them. That changed when I opened the door and exposed them to the rank smell, followed by the realisation of the horrors into which they would soon be advancing. How I kept my food down, I do not know, and perversely, I felt some sympathy for what my boots were now being subjected to. If only Sid knew how I was treating his prized parade ground boots. Suffice to say that he would have been mortified, but since this would be the very last time I would wear these boots, I couldn't have cared less. At the end of the night, my boots were going to be consigned to the rubbish bin.

Attack team 2 entered through the side gate and managed to stay on their feet by holding each other's hands the same as children do when performing a nursery rhyme dance. Paul Simon's song 'Slip sliding away' could have been written for us as we slipped this way and that as quietly as we could into our allotted attack position. Strangely, no one wanted to sit down and rest whilst we waited.

Locard's theory relates to the exchange of particles between two objects. Basically, 'when two objects meet, there is an exchange of matter from one to the other'. This exchange principle is essential when looking for evidence. In this operation, that exchange of matter took on another meaning as our boots fought a losing battle with the offending poo in an effort to prevent collateral damage from occurring to our tunic trousers. Holding each other's hands certainly helped us keep upright, but how no-one fell head over heels, I do not know – perhaps a divine presence was looking after us. Attack team 2 was quite literally up to their necks in smelly stuff awaiting the attack command, which thankfully came through.

When the command 'Attack, Attack' came over the radio, we slow stepped our way, slipping and sliding continually to the back door and forced entry. Not a difficult task as the door had been left unlocked. Inside, though, the place was packed so tightly with people literally pressed against each wall, so tight in fact that sardines in a tin had more space to move around. Either way, we needed to enter, so we forced our way into the backroom in the process, packing the people even tighter together against the external walls.

If the occupants weren't a couple before, they certainly were now. Progress was slow but constant, and after a time, we met up with our colleagues entering through the front door. The premises were secured, after which our traffic division officers armed with the specialist 'Dragon light' joined us and turned them on. The room lit up like Blackpool illuminations, making the room very hot and stuffy in a matter of seconds and taking away our night vision in the process. When they worked, these lights were the business, but since the drain on the batteries was so great, they only lasted minutes before suddenly failing without notice. This happened after about five minutes, after which the room went pitch black. Fortunately, during those five minutes of light, I could see that the floor was covered in disgusting smelly stuff presumably brought in from the outside that was now intertwined with an assortment of drugs, knives, stolen property, cans, bottles and glasses lying on the floor.

My parents should have named me 'Lucky' as I had now been treated to a win double – the first was bad enough walking through the back yard full of smelly stuff, and the second being my role as exhibits officer where it was down to me to get hands-on recovering evidence from the floor.

Not wanting to give the baddies a laugh at my predicament, I waited until all of them had been removed before I systematically started to search the premises, seizing items as I went and preserving them for evidence.

Suffice to say; it was a long smelly night interspersed with spells out in the road breathing in car fumes – a far better proposition than the alternative. I persevered with this until the search was complete and laden with my 'Evidence' I returned to the station, where the exhibits were sealed, registered in book 66, and locked away in the property store.

By the end of this, I was in such a smelly disgusting state that the early turn station officer took pity on me and, using a broom to keep me at arm's length, he ushered me into the back of the station van, where as 'Billy no mates' I dejectedly sat on a bench. A short while later, the driver arrived and, with doors wide open, drove me to the Drum car park where I was unceremoniously dumped. During the ride, I managed to untie my boot laces (not a pleasant job), and after getting out of the van, I kicked them off my feet and threw them into the waste bin. Decency prevented me from doing the same with my trousers, but as soon as I could, they followed my boots a short time later.

It was only after doing that that I treated myself to a well-earned steaming hot bath followed by a well-earned good sleep. 45

---ooo0ooo---

Chapter 9

Dog Handler

A few days later, I started an early turn tour walking around my post in the Southwark Park Road area. Whilst on patrol; I was confronted by a member of the public who had found a stray mongrel dog not dissimilar to 'Tramp' in Disney's Lady and the Tramp. I tried and failed dismally to recall dealing with the dogs' lecture and the dog finding scenario that I had completed at Hendon. This was tricky – now I seemed to recall that stray dogs had to be taken to the station, where they were placed in the station kennel, entered into a book and then collected by Battersea Dogs Home maybe. I had to take decisive action and fast. The dog had no collar or lead, so unless he followed my commands, how was I going to get the dog to the back yard of the station and into the dog kennels.

That's when I had a Eureka moment. Thinking outside the box, I considered what I had on me that I could use as a collar and lead, and that's when I remembered my leather belt, currently holding my trousers up. I took it off and, using it as a collar; I placed it over the dog's head. Now with one hand holding up my trousers and the other holding my makeshift dog lead, I walked the dog through the streets to

Tower Bridge Police Station, where I placed it into the station kennel. Job done.

As I entered the front office, I was well pleased with the innovative way I had dealt with this new and demanding everyday problem, especially as it was without any input from my fellow colleagues. That lasted all for about a minute when I reported what I had done to the station officer, who looked at me incredulously and said, 'You did what? Do you know what that means? Well, do you?'

In all innocence, I replied 'No'.

The station officer went on, 'Well, you're about to learn' He took hold of a large book and threw it at me. 'Firstly, check that there are no reports in that book of any dog with that description having been reported lost. If there is, contact the owner and get them to pick it up as soon as possible. If there is no report, make one out, giving the dogs full descriptive details. After you've done that, arrange for a dog found tele printer message to be sent to all surrounding stations, and oh, don't forget to make sure the dog is fed and watered. Once you've done that, come back and see me.'

So instead of walking around my beat for the next few hours, I was sorting out the paperwork to report a lost dog. I learnt that it was a ridiculous amount of paperwork for something so simple. After a few hours completing all the paperwork, I went out to feed and water the dog as ordered. I opened the kennel door to place the bowl of food and water on the floor when the bloody thing escaped into the yard and out through the gate, never to be seen again. I reported back to the station officer, who, after laughing, told me to update the dog found book, and send a cancel dog found message to the surrounding stations. The end result was a whole shift dealing with the paperwork for 'the dog that never was'.

Funnily enough, I never dealt with another dog found for the remainder of my service – once bitten, twice shy - told you I was a fast learner.

Chapter 10

Rock Hard Pork Pies and Tea

The Grunwick dispute was a two-year strike that lasted from 1976 through to 1978. It started before I joined the police and was still going strong when I was posted to Tower Bridge Police Station. It was no surprise then that this was to be the first of many operational tours I would be involved in. The most distressing part of this was getting up just after midnight, arriving at Tower Bridge by 2 am where we would board a coach to our feeding station at Wembley Section House. The term feeding station is a bit of an exaggeration. Our breakfast was timed for 3 am, waiting patiently in a long queue snaking around the section house car park to grab a cup of tea and a cold rock hard pork pie from a police mobile refreshment van with a call sign of 'Teapot 500.'

Once fed and watered, our serial was deployed as containment outside the front gates of the Grunwick factory, standing in the kerb between the animated demonstrators on the footpath and the roadway leading to the entrance gates. Coaches used this roadway to carry those employees not on strike (considered by some as 'Scabs') into the factory to work.

Policing demonstrations was, to say the least, in its infancy, with barriers, proper equipment and shield trained officers some years into the future. We would do our best to keep the Queen's Peace, locking arms as ordered to form a human barrier despite our lack of training. The idea was that by acting as a human fence, we would be able to keep the demonstrators penned on the footpath away from the coaches using the roadway.

Everything was fairly orderly until the police were ordered to link arms and shuffle together, a sure sign that the coaches carrying scab workers were not far away. That's when the demonstrators started to surge forward, probing the linked police arm barrier for weakness as it pushed this way and that a bit like the Mexican wave at football matches.

With our backs to the crowd, we could see the coaches as they came into view, and sure enough, the surge increased correspondingly with our backs to the demonstrators, we were pretty vulnerable to unseen assaults, which is where our supervising sergeants and inspectors came into their own looking after our backs and wellbeing.

Like Meerkats, they stood immediately in front of us facing the opposition head-on, with their eyes scanning everywhere to ensure we were not being subjected to any sly acts of underhand violence.

We, in turn, responded in kind to the barked commands of 'Push', and supported by our sergeants and inspectors, the linked arm fence would stretch and contract in unison. The impressive part was that I never once saw the linked arm police barrier ever give way except to allow access and egress to officers arresting demonstrators.

To cries of 'Push-me – Pull-me' to all intents and purposes, I could have been auditioning for a role in Dr. Doolittle.

Needless to say, I would be seconded to the Grunwick aid on many more occasions over the coming months, and every time it would pretty much follow in the same manner. For me, it was quite a gentle introduction to demonstrations as apart from the pushing, pulling and shouting, I never experienced outright violence at Grunwicks, unlike some of the other demonstrations that were to follow.

---ooo0ooo---

Chapter 11

Siege of Oswin Street

Violence was something I was to experience a couple of times in my first few months. Sadly, during my police journey, it would sit alongside me like a permanent undercurrent manifesting itself without notice at various times.

The first violent act was directed against a probationer PC I knew as Dave, based at Southwark police station in the Borough High Street. Dave had passed through training school a few weeks before me, and through the lottery of life had been posted to Southwark whilst I had been posted to Tower Bridge. Southwark police station (phonetically known as Mike Delta) used the same radio frequency as Tower Bridge (Mike Tango) and Rotherhithe (Mike Romeo) police stations. This meant we could liaise directly with officers from all stations via the personal radio.

One night duty, a call for "urgent assistance' was transmitted by Dave over the personal radio link. Any call for "urgent assistance' meant a colleague needed urgent help or was in serious trouble, and so, everyone nearby responded as fast as they could. To increase the police response capability, the call was also circulated via the main set radio, resulting in vehicles from surrounding stations turning on the "blues and twos' to be first on the scene.

On arrival at the scene, Dave was found holding his hands over his face covering several cuts from cheek to jowl made by some dirtbag with a craft like knife. The dirtbag had well and truly disappeared into the ether by the time any help arrived. After initial 1st aid at the scene, an ambulance was called, and Dave was taken immediately to a hospital for treatment.

It transpired that Dave had spotted a suspect acting suspiciously. He decided for some reason not to notify the station reserve of what he was about to do. He followed the dirtbag into the labyrinth of small alleys behind the Elephant & Castle shopping centre, which is where Dave stopped him.

In the course of the subsequent search, Dave failed to notice the open craft knife he was carrying secreted in one of his hands that at such close quarters he used to maximum effect to cause serious facial damage.

Apart from the physical scars an assault like this-must cause some psychological damage, and it was no great surprise to me that I learnt a few weeks later that Dave had put his papers in and left the police force for good.

I took on board from this episode to always keep in touch with the station and check hands for weapons before moving in close to a suspect.

My baptism of violence occurred about two months later. I had been out of Hendon for about three months practising some of the things I had been taught. Luckily I had not been required to stop a running horse or give the 4-minute warning, but I had had a few arrests - mainly drunks under my belt, and had searched an illegal club and dealt with a lost dog.

Up to then, I had not had to defend myself against attack. That changed one-night duty when I was sent with Vulch and officers from other surrounding stations to assist Southwark police officers contain a house in Oswin Street, currently occupied by a well-known family of persistent offenders. When we arrived, a siege situation had developed. We controlled the outside, whilst the occupants controlled the inside – a sort of status quo.

The so-called siege started when, for reasons, only the address residents understood a decision was made by them to use the cover of darkness to burn plastic insulation off a quantity of stolen cabling. The area chosen to do this was in their back garden. It is not surprising that the smell of burning and the resulting thick black smoke attracted attention from a member of the public who reported it to the police. A policeman was subsequently sent to investigate, where he observed what was happening and thought to himself

"Hello, hello, hello – what's going on here then' or something similar to that.

Up to now – normal police work.

Those initial attending officers, had they suspected an arrestable offence was being committed, could have immediately used their powers of 'entry and arrest.' They chose not to do so and decided to summon police reinforcements to the scene. The time it took for police reinforcements to arrive allowed the whole family to retreat into their home, where they started the process of fortifying it to protect against any coming police search. It was now a standoff between police and the house occupants, so the late senior, Superintendent Roberts, was called out to take operational command.

Prior to our arrival, the address was surrounded by about 20 police constables, four or more sergeants, two inspectors and now a Superintendent. With the other officers arriving from the outlying stations, that number swelled exponentially.

Vulch and I arrived and were briefed as to what was happening. Basically, as was obvious from the slurred taunts being hurled from the address, the occupants had consumed copious amounts of alcohol and were now drunk. A vicious circle developed where drunkenness fuelled their bravado, which led to increasingly vulgar insults being hurled out the house windows. The situation was spiraling – not a good position to negotiate from.

The police at that time had the post-war Dixon of Dock Green' mentality where officers were expected to go around dressed in their standard police tunic, wearing a cork helmet secured to the head by a thin chin strap continually saying Evening all' to all and sundry. Unfortunately, the uniform had not significantly changed with the times and pretty much remained the same as it had been back then. As I was about to find out, the police uniform was not surrounded by a magical force field, and it was most definitely not suited for the task that was about to unfold.

With the house now well and truly contained, no one could escape and get away, and conversely, we could not get in. A Mexican standoff developed, which the Superintendent was not happy about. So to jolly things along, the Superintendent authorised an application for a search warrant and sent a police officer off to get it. This took some time to arrange, so just in case it was needed, he sent off to the station for some equipment used in dealing with violent mental patients – the one and only station shield.

Today riot shields are readily available for use on demand, but back in 1977, that was not the case. Back then, the only equipment available was this lone ranger mental health shield. It was not see-through like those used today, although there was a clear 6-inch by 2-inch pop-riveted viewing window within the pale blue metal shield about three-quarters of the way up ~~to~~ on its front panel. Side protection was provided by curved flanges to each side. Its design was pretty identical in shape and size to the Scutum shield used centuries before by Roman legionaries, and boy, it was as heavy as hell. The night duty CID, Crampo and Bonny Lad arrived on the scene just as officers returned with the 'mental health shield.

They entered into a discussion with the Superintendent as we waited patiently for the warrant to arrive. Once we had it, the Superintendent requested the occupants to come out of the premises, a demand met by a chorus of calls such as Come and get us you bunch of nice people if you dare.' The words used rhymed more with punt, so it was not very polite, to put it mildly. As far as the Superintendent was concerned, enough was enough. Now, no more Mr. Nice Guy, he intended to make an example and end it, so ordered us to force entry.

The plan was simple. Entry was a two-pronged attack via the front door and a first-floor garden window. The front wooden door was set back in a brick porch and had a glass fanlight, and it was to this door that, along with a few other officers, I was told to force entry through.

As we launched this attack, Percy and a group of other officers used borrowed extending-ladders to attempt entry into the rear first-floor bedroom windows.

Crampo and Bonny Lad stood back and watched, waiting to follow on once the premises were secured. They would have still been waiting today, as when we body charged the front door, it never budged – not an inch. So there we were huddled in a big group outside the door when suddenly the fan glass was broken from within, and one of the occupants was throwing shards of glass through the fanlight right on top of us. Now it didn't take a brain surgeon to realise that whoever that person was, they were either extremely tall or standing on something behind the door.

The frontal attack pretty much faltered because try as we might, we could not force the door. We found out later it had a kitchen item, something like a fridge, freezer or washing machine stacked behind it, which, apart from barring the door, gave the inmates an excellent platform to stand on and shower us with glass shards.

To protect me from the glass shards, I wore a cork helmet secured with a chin strap. It was as useful as a chocolate teaspoon in doing the job it was supposed to do. I found that out the hard way when one of the shards went through my eyelid and punctured my right eye. Luckily I had blinked my eyelid before the glass shard hit, which protected my eye from taking the full force – otherwise, I would have lost my eye.

Nevertheless, the impact hurt like hell, and with blood now flowing freely down my face, I was led away from the front door by a woman officer affectionately known as Keyhole Kate to a place of safety alongside the station van, where first aid was provided. My role in this was now that of a one-eyed observer.

That's when Crampo and Bonny Lad rose to the occasion. Realising that the front door was a no, no, they made an instant decision, took up the mental health shield from its resting place and used it to shield them as they jumped through ground floor bay window straight into the front room; completely destroying them in the process. The premises had been breached, and Crampo and Bonny Lad were followed by Vulch and a PC I knew as Allan. Timing is everything, and sod's law saw Allan ~~as~~ being the the fourth police officer to enter the front room. As he exited the front room into the hallway, one of the occupants chopped him in the leg with a garden spade, catching him just below the knee cap with such force that it almost completely severed it from the rest of his leg. It is strange how the fickle finger of fate had suddenly chosen Allan as its next victim. So with two of the frontal assault team hospitalised, things couldn't get worse – could they?

Nine police hurt in house raid

NINE policemen were injured yesterday during a raid by uniformed officers in the early hours of the morning on a house in Oswin-st., Southwark.

The raid, which followed a period of police observation on the house, was led by Superintendent Norman Roberts of Southwark police, who said yesterday that nine of the dozen officers involved had received cuts and bruises from " missiles " hurled from the house.

Six people were yesterday helping Southwark police with their inquiries into the recovery of stolen property.

Well, as a matter of fact, they could. As part of the rear garden attack team, Percy was the first person to start climbing the ladder to a first-floor bedroom window, which is when he was hit on the head by a thrown paint pot, causing him to fall off the ladder and suffer serious injury in the process.

Whichever way you looked at it, the operation was going badly wrong with the police at present coming off a poor second.

It was whilst waiting for the ambulance to arrive that the female occupant Mrs. B a self-declared witch, was brought out of the house. Sadly she was no shrinking violet and definitely not a role model for the younger generation

Mrs. B was ranting and raving as she was brought forcefully from the building, during which her ranting climaxed with her cursing with all her witch powers that every police officer present would all be dead in 6 months. Good job. I'm not a sensitive person as this could be quite upsetting – six months to live better get a drink in quick then.

Looking back, I can say that no police officer involved in the siege dropped dead within six months – either because

a) police officers are blessed with thick curse proof skins or
b) Mrs. B had not paid her witches club membership, so her curses bank was not in credit or
c) more probably because Mrs. B was talking a load of B-ll-cks.

The score at the end of the day was breathtaking – on the one side, three police officers were hospitalized, a further six suffered lesser injuries, whilst on the other side, and six persons had been arrested. It was certainly not an unmitigated success story, and for me, it could quite easily have been the end of my police career.

As for my injuries, the cause of the bleeding was a cut to my right eyelid that required two stitches. The real damage was caused to my right eye, which the glass shard had punctured right through to the vitreous humor – Ouch. After emergency treatment, I was told the extent of the injury to my eye would not be fully known for about two weeks, so during that time I wore an eye patch dressing looking more like a pirate than a policeman. It was a long wait.

With being off work, I started to reflect on my first few months in the police and especially back to my initial meeting with the Superintendent at Tower Bridge. Maybe he was right.....perhaps I wouldn't last long in the police.

I reprimanded myself. Sod it, I thought; this was not the time for doubts – and with that, I resolved there and then to prove him wrong. The two weeks passed, and before I knew it, the patch was off my eye, and the doctors gave me their verdicts. Thankfully although my eye had been damaged, the damage was such that it did not prevent me from continuing my job as a police officer. Boy, I was one happy bunny – best have a drink to celebrate.

The subsequent court case held at the Old Bailey was a blast and a bit like the search didn't go quite as we hoped. Vulch gave his evidence, which basically saw him as a superhero crime-fighting cop – perhaps Superman in disguise because seeing what he saw would have required x-ray vision.

In his evidence Vulch positively identified person 'A' as the man behind the door throwing the glass shard that caused my injuries, after which he identified person 'B' as the culprit swinging the spade that caused Allan's injuries and to cap it all as a sort of coup de grace Vulch also managed to run upstairs into the rear bedroom in time to see person 'C' throwing the paint pot through the window that caused Percy's injuries. Vulch's evidence was ripped to pieces by the Defence Counsel, who quite rightly used it to discredit all the police versions of the event.

Needless to say, the defendants were cleared of assault charges although found guilty and sentenced to prison terms for various theft and public order offences.

Today this type of search quite rightly in these circumstances would not have taken place unless someone's life was in extreme danger. It would now be a waiting game, allowing time for the occupants to sober up and come to their senses, after which they would have walked out. No one would have been injured, and the job would have been.

During my service; hindsight was a wonderful process that I found to be a double-edged sword. Dynamic situations require instant decisions. Provided that decision goes well, great, but if it doesn't, someone will take months to review that decision and then use that review to question why a particular decision was made.

People often fail to realise that persons making decisions in the heat of the moment do not have that period of reflective review. So now, after 37 years of reflecting on this case, in hindsight, it was the wrong course of action to take but be that as it may, I do not hold the police responsible for my injuries – 'c'est la vie.'

So what did I learn – I learnt not to have Vulch as a witness, that's for sure. I also started to realise the importance of quality evidence and proper planning – two things missing on this occasion.

---oooOooo---

Chapter 12

Miracle Man

As a police probationer, I was required to learn about performing station duties that mainly covered three areas.

The first was that of gaoler whereby you were responsible to the charge room sergeant for looking after the prisoners.

The second was to assist the station officer in the front office interfacing with people attending the station front counter to report accidents, crimes, lost property, and of course, lost / found dogs, etc

Whilst the third posting was to perform reserve officer functions such as looking after the telephone and teleprinter calls, allocating calls to patrol officers and acting as a pivotal control point to direct officers in most emergencies. The one exception being in the event of a nuclear attack where I would abandon my position, run to the Anchor tap and find a secure place in the basement alongside the beer.

There was a fourth posting you could be sent to, which depended upon staffing levels at the Willow Walk car pound, which just happened to be on our manner. Thankfully not a regular event. When required to do this posting, it was a sure-fire recipe to be bored silly or hone up your confrontational management skills by arguing with some outraged car owner.

The injuries I received to my eye meant I was off work for about a month. On my return to normal relief duties, I guess my supervisors felt sorry for me or something like that as they gently eased me back into work, and to keep an eye on me, so to speak, I was posted as the early duty gaoler by the relief inspector where I worked closely alongside the charge room sergeant. In this capacity; ⸺I first met 'Moon,' a plainclothes crime squad officer working alongside the station CID.

Moon entered the charge room door ushering in a prisoner who appeared to be in some pain and distress as he walked with the aid of two crutches slowly across the charge room towards the wooden bench, whereupon he unceremoniously collapsed in a heap, and his crutches fell onto the charge room floor. The prisoner's name was Peter. Moon had arrested Peter, a local druggie and everyday scoundrel because he had failed to appear at court to answer a production of cannabis charge, leading to the court issuing a no-bail arrest warrant, which had led to police attending Peter's home address in Rotherhithe and arresting him on it.

A minute or so after Peter arrived the charge room, Sergeant Mushy Peas entered and prepared to document the prisoner. In accordance with police procedure, he was obliged to hear the arresting officer's evidence of arrest, so looking at Peter, he said, 'Listen to what this officer has to say.'

Moon - 'Right Sarge - I attended Peter's address in Lower Road. The door was opened by Peter's girlfriend, Kim. We entered, and I saw Peter, a person I personally know. Peter is wanted on a no-bail warrant issued by Tower Bridge Magistrates Court for the production of cannabis. I arrested and cautioned him, to which he replied, 'Mr. Mooney, I could not attend court due to injuries; as you can see, I can only now get about with the use of crutches'. Peter asked his girlfriend Kim to contact a solicitor, and after getting dressed, with the aid of crutches, he made his way into the station van and was brought directly here.'

Mushy Peas said to Peter, 'Is that correct' to which Peter, still seated, replied 'Yes.'

Peter remained seated on the bench whilst Mushy Peas took his details and entered them onto the book 12 charge sheet (Now known as a custody record). Whilst this documentation was being written, the charge room phone rang, which was answered by Moon.   He had a brief conversation with the caller, after which he turned to Peter and said, 'It's Kim – she wants to speak to you.'

Peter didn't give it a second thought as he stood up unaided from the charge room bench, and with his crutches still lying on the floor, he walked straight over to Moon, took the phone from his extended hand and held it to his ear. Peter started talking to Kim in a low voice. He had been so engrossed talking to her for a minute or so that he never saw Moon walk over and pick up Peter's crutches, which he was now holding. It was only when he turned around to see a smiling Moon holding them that Peter realized he had made an error and without pausing, he spoke into the phone saying 'Kim, my love, I seem to have made a bit of a booboo.' Game over.

Needless to say, Peter walked over to the court without the aid of his crutches and was dealt with accordingly.

If I were being cynical, I'd think Peter was trying to have one over on the police and the judiciary, but if not, it is a reminder that miracles still happen and proof that they can occur in the strangest of places.

As for Moon, this was our first meeting but was not to be our last. I was destined to meet up and work in plain clothes closely with him on various squads throughout my police service.

During my gaoler attachments, one other person I met was a very distant relative of mine, perhaps two or three generations separating us. He came from the Vauxhall side of the family whilst I came from the North London side. I took the opportunity to speak to him whilst he was languishing in the cells awaiting an interview for a theft-related matter. We had been brought up with a different set of values that straddled each side of the legal versus illegal spectrum. This was our one and only conversation; it certainly wasn't a case of having a family get together, that's for sure. It wasn't that long after we met that I heard he had drowned trying to swim the Thames fully clothed. If nothing else, that clearly demonstrated which side of my family was gifted with a brain cell or two? I leave you to decide who that was…

---ooo0ooo---

Chapter 13

Accident or no accident

I was posted to the front office to assist the station officer one day. It was not a busy day, so I was reading a paper and minding my own business when Bam Bam came on the radio giving a running commentary of a foot chase he was having with a local thief. Bam Bam was not a member of my relief, but on this day, he was working with us under the compulsory working rest day rules - a requirement which saw police officers from other reliefs work alongside each other on an infrequent basis.

Bam Bam was as tall as he was wide, and with him being in the Metropolitan Police 1st 15 rugby team, he was extremely fit. Bam Bam's physique could best be described as having arms like Popeye with a body shape similar to that of 'Odd Job' from the James Bond 'Goldfinger' movie. Bam Bam was always grinning, a trademark feature that he maintained for all his service, and for some reason, he always wore a pair of hobnail boots I suspect bought from the local army surplus store, which were used by soldiers.

On this occasion, Bam Bam was patrolling in the Tower Bridge Road area when he happened upon a thief. The offence committed has been lost in the mists of time, but the young, slim thief wore trainers and as fit as a flea fancying his chances of escape against Bam Bam had it on his dancers.

It never went the way our thief thought it would, as Bam Bam started to match him stride for stride, high and low they both went with the only constant sound being the clack, clack, clack inexorably getting closer and closer as Bam Bam's hobnails came into contact with the ground.

That sound must have been a bit disconcerting for the thief who could see himself slowly losing this race, which is when he took the last throw of the dice and taking his life in his hands he haphazardly ran out in front of the Tower Bridge Road traffic, somehow, more by luck than judgment getting safely across the road to the other side.

Unfortunately for him, Bam Bam followed. Bam Bam was not as lucky as our thief because in crossing the road, he ran smack bang into the front side wing of a moving car leaving the imprint of a thigh mark in the wing panel. Rolling around the front of the car, and without stopping to exchange names and addresses, Bam Bam continued chasing the thief who he eventually captured in the aptly named Crucifix Lane. That was where Bam Bam summarily splatted him against a wall in a cross position, searched and arrested him. The station van was dispatched to collect Bam Bam and his prisoner, and with the excitement over, I went back to reading my paper.

That was until an irate motorist came in to complain about a failure to stop accident where the perpetrator was described as being an unknown policeman looking like Odd job. It did not take a brain surgeon to work out whose car Bam Bam had just dented.

Now it was debatable as to whether this was a reportable traffic accident. No personal injury had been caused to either the driver or Bam Bam, and at best, it was a name and addresses exchanged job. With that in mind, I took the drivers details, created a G9 accident claims record, the reference number and a contact telephone number I gave to the driver for him to make direct contact and arrange payment for the repairs, which in these circumstances would be unreservedly paid.

As for Bam Bam, he was in the charge room a little later still grinning– none the worse for his exertions.

---ooo0ooo---

Chapter 14

Station Groupies

The number of groupies who follow rock and movie stars is well documented. The groupies who become fascinated by men in uniform are not so well documented. Once the prey has been chosen, the groupies do all they can to bring themselves to their notice? That was the case with Debbie and Nadine, two local girls who started stalking a fair few of my fellow colleagues based at Tower Bridge Police Station.

Debbie and Nadine commenced their attack by innocently coming over to the station's front office normally on night duty, where they both remained for a couple of hours literally standing on the public side of the front office counter talking to individual police officers as they came into the front office for some reason or other. This, in turn, led to a playful banter developing whereby officers were invited over to their flat across the road from the station to partake in some tea and crumpet, which the girls offered to supply, free of charge.

Let me be quite clear about this: I did not partake in this kind of offer, but I know a few who did. The feedback they provided was that they weren't too fazed about the tea, but the crumpet portion supplied was more than sufficient to sate the appetite of a hungry police officer. By all accounts, the crumpet portions were served hot and steamy, which left those sampling wanting more and more – something that caused more than a few 'handbag at dawn' duels between officers who felt they were being sidelined. I wouldn't want you to think this was anything like the antics in 'Debby does Dallas,' although clearly there were some similarities. Needless to say, when senior management heard about the trouble caused by this freebie, the spoilsports put a stop to it.

---ooo0ooo---

Chapter 15

Rubberbum

Rubberbum was an officer who made so many errors that he became a standing joke across the four reliefs, and I think it is fair to say that Rubberbum was not gifted with an overabundance of common sense.

Rubberbum was the epitome of the blundering constable Dogberry from Shakespeare's 'Much ado about nothing.' The caricature of Dogberry is of someone with a physique like an inverted S – with a bulging stomach counterbalanced by an equally bulbous behind. The character and description could have been Rubberbum to a T.

To preserve Rubberbums dignity; I will refer to him as PC 2½.

Rubberbum was so well known that whenever he used the personal radio call into the station, from out of nowhere, a voice would respond with a reverberating 'RRRRRRRRRRRR' caused by the tongue vibrating with the roof of the mouth followed a short while later with 'Rubberbum.'

Luckily, personal radios used then were not uniquely identifiable, unlike the ones used today, so who said what could be surmised but not absolutely proved. In the police, playing pranks was a way of life, especially on a probationer where you could perhaps be sent to a hardware store and told to get a jar of elbow grease, or sent to an undertaker and told there was a body in it for them (in this instance a play on words body being slang for arrest).

Pranks in the main were propagated through the station's reserve officer. After all was said and done, messages were passed on to patrolling officers from this nerve centre. Experienced police officers usually filled this role, and they were pretty good at gilding the lily and making it believable.

One night duty PC 2 1/2 's relief decided to play a prank on him. The reserve officer turned the teleprinter off and prepared a false teleprinter message that looked like the real McCoy. He printed off the message and handed it to the relief sergeant to pass on to Rubberbum when the relief paraded.

The spoofed message purportedly sent to Mike Tango from Information Room (IR) looked real and went something like this:

MT from IR

'It is suspected that a contagious form of bacteria is being spread in Bird droppings.'

The Metropolitan Police have been requested to take bird dropping samples from Tower Bridge starting at midnight tonight and hourly thereafter until 6 am.

Samples are to be sealed and entered in book 66, awaiting collection from a government agency.'

IR reference 1977/1/2345

The relief sergeant passed the teleprinter message to PC 2½ to deal with during the relief briefing when it paraded at 09.45 pm. Now had Rubberbum considered this for a moment, he would have known that this was a relief wind. The first clue was that jurisdiction for policing Tower Bridge lay with the City Police, not the Metropolitan Police, so any request, if made, would have been sent directly to them, and secondly because the relief was sniggering as the briefing ended, and everyone went their merry way.

Luckily, this night duty was pretty quiet, and apart from a few radio checks to make sure he was OK, not a whisper was heard from Rubberbum either at refreshments or tea breaks until he resurfaced after the rest of his relief had returned to the station and been sent home.

The reason Rubberbum was late was because he had diligently patrolled up and down Tower Bridge the whole night recovering samples of bird pooh, which he had stored separately in several used Bryant and May matchboxes. The teleprinter message stated that the last sample was to be taken at 6 am, which he did. Once that sample had been taken, Rubberbum returned to the station to deposit all the samples, each containing the time and exact location on the bridge where they had been recovered.

To continue the prank, Rubberbums relief had passed details of the wind up on to the early turn station officer. Keeping the prank going when Rubberbum appeared, the station officer made him seal the bird pooh samples in exhibit bags, enter their details into the book 66 (a universal station record for various items of property), and hand them back to him for placing in the secure stores' cupboard.

It's no surprise then that as Rubberbum left the station to go home and sleep, those exhibits along with the Book 66 entries were promptly deposited into the station rubbish bin.

Rubberbum, to this day, probably still thinks his bird pooh exhibits helped prevent the spread of some contagious bacteria across the UK.

As Tower Bridges operational nerve centre, the reserve room was strategically placed between the station office and the collator's room. The collator's room contained local intelligence reports, so was where the reliefs paraded before each shift. These three offices formed a natural meeting place where oncoming relief officers would meet with the outgoing relief and discuss updates on recent events.

It was into this collective meeting place that I reported for work one-night duty and talked to the outgoing reserve officer. During our conversation, Rubberbum's voice came over the radio.

PC 2½ – 'Mike Tango, Mike Tango, stop in the street name check please.'

Reserve officer – 'PC 2½ – are you alone.'

PC 2½   – 'No, I'm with PC XYZ'. PC XYZ was known by the nickname 'leatherneck' and according to their own fellow relief officers, PC2½ and XYZ were a unique double-act sharing a combined IQ of about 1, and that was erring on the generous side.

Reserve officer – 'PC 2½ give your location and go ahead.'

PC 2½ – 'Lower Road outside Surrey Docks Station,' after which he gave the individuals name, date of birth, gender and ethnicity

Reserve officer – 'PC 2½ are you free to speak' - Now, when the comment 'Are you free to speak' is made; it means there is some information known about the individual that the reserve officer is about to pass on to you.

PC 2½ – 'Mike Tango – yes, yes – go ahead.'

Reserve officer – 'PC 2½ - the details given show your person to be wanted for burglary'

PC 2½ – 'Mike Tango – he says he's not wanted – are you sure.'

Reserve officer – 'PC 2½ does he have a scar on his chin.'

PC 2½ – 'Mike Tango – that's a no – he has a full beard.'

Reserve Officer – 'PC 2½, Have you checked whether the scar is beneath the beard.'

PC 2½ then started screaming into the personal radio – 'Mike Tango, Mike Tango chasing suspect …'

After we had picked ourselves up off the floor, we went to assist PC 2½ - after all, he was sadly one of us.

I can safely say that although Rubberbum and I were posted to the same station and saw each other pretty much on a regular basis, we never worked together.

---ooo0ooo--

Chapter 16

Who Stole My Glasses?

Botty was an experienced police officer who was posted as 'A' relief's permanent reserve / assistant station officer. We would occasionally relieve him of these duties for a day or so to provide him with firstly a break and secondly to allow us the newbies to learn what the role entailed. It was while I was completing this posting one day that Steff the incoming reserve officer arrived to relieve me. There was nothing unusual about this particular day other than I was about to be accused of theft.

Now Steff was a large likeable lady with a disproportionate set of assets that even a reinforced bra had difficulty supporting, and despite the best efforts, her assets quite literally dropped down to rest alongside her belly button. Although Steff was normally a good-natured officer, if she thought you were taking the proverbial, she was known to occasionally get out of her pram. If that happened, then you'd better watch out as she could be a little volatile, something her long-suffering husband George was only too aware of. Steff stood in front of me, removed her reading glasses from her head, and started pulling her hair back. The glasses she was wearing she put on top of the reserve room table, and once she had sorted herself out, I stood up and allowed her to sit in the reserve officer's seat. She sat down and started adjusting it to make herself as comfortable as possible with her ample assets lying fully supported along the length of the reserve officer's desk.

I talked through the outstanding messages with her as there were a couple that her relief would need to attend, but otherwise, nothing to write home about. As I was about to leave, I saw Steff looking for her glasses but couldn't find them to read the messages in more detail. As the only other person in the reserve room at that time, she wrongly assumed that I had taken them and was playing a prank, so she said to me, "Okay, Daisy, give me my glasses back."

I said, "Steff, I don't have your glasses, honest."

She looked at me and said, "Daisy, don't get me angry; just give me my glasses back."

I again replied, "Steff, I don't have your glasses, honest."

Steff's whole manner changed as she slowly began to rise from her seat. It was clear from her tone of voice as she repeated, "Daisy, don't get me angry," that Steff was starting to get annoyed. This was not a good place to be. Luckily, as Steff stood up, her glasses that had become embedded in the underside of her assets fell out onto the tabletop. *Phew, nice timing.* Steff had been blissfully unaware that her reading glasses had been embedded into her charms, sort of cocooned and safely wrapped.

As soon as they fell onto the table, I pointed to them and chipped in, "Steff, yours, I believe." Steff's face was a picture; I don't know about fifty shades of grey, but I can certainly say it went fifty shades of red, finally settling on beetroot. Steff could still speak, though, because as I made good my escape, I heard her calling after me, "If you say anything about this, Daisy, you'll suffer." Despite the threats, I told my relief, and like a wildfire, word soon got around the station.

Luckily for me, Steff could see the funny side of it and never did anything to make me suffer. It just shows how easy it is to jump to conclusions and make unfounded allegations; it seems to be something that continues to this day.

---ooo0ooo--

Chapter 17

Death

Death is something we all have to experience at some time in our lives, and yet, at 22 years of age, I had never seen a lifeless body. As a police officer, it was something I had to learn to deal with.

My introduction to death was arranged within the first few weeks of my posting to Tower Bridge. I was sent to meet the police coroner's officer at Guy's Hospital mortuary, where I was taken through to the sharp end and introduced to the mortician. A mortician is someone who assists the pathologist during post-mortems and, apart from doing most of the grisly donkey work, maintains the cleanliness of the mortuary tools, tables, and body gurneys. One thing I remember was the mortuary smelt of carbolic, a smell that remains with me to this day. Not nice!

"So, you've never seen a dead body before," he said, walking past an empty gurney with a wooden neck rest, waiting for the next occupant to arrive as we headed towards rows of refrigerator-type doors embedded into the walls. "The last officer who came here was sick on the floor; I hope you won't do that. I don't like my clean floor getting dirty." We made our way to a refrigerator door which he promptly pulled a freezer compartment open inside of which was a plastic Tupperware box lying on top of an empty gurney. He removed the Tupperware box, opened the lid, and offered me a sandwich from it. Naturally, I politely refused, but the mortician removed one himself and took a bite. Apparently, this was his idea of a joke, which I didn't think was very funny. Morticians are a strange lot. Joke over; I was then taken to a refrigerator with a real cadaver. He opened the refrigerator and removed the body and gurney out into the mortuary so I could see at first hand the end results of his preparatory handiwork. Not a pretty sight!

I apparently got off light with my introduction to death. It was not the same for everybody, though. In one prank, an officer with a reputation for being a wind-up merchant (officer B) thought it would be good fun if he got into a refrigerated container and waited for the probationer to arrive. The idea was for the supposedly dead body to sit up on being pulled from the refrigerator, causing the probationer to quite rightly scream his head off - Clearly, the timing was critical.

Unfortunately, this was a prank with a twist. With the connivance of the mortician, a second officer (Officer A) had already been placed into a refrigerated container next to where Officer B was being placed. It was total darkness when the refrigerator door closed on Officer B.

Allowing sufficient time for the relief to quietly enter the mortuary, "Officer A' suddenly said, "It's fucking cold in here," causing Officer B to understandably freak out. With the laughter of his relief still ringing in his ears, officer B never played a prank like this again.

Mortuaries were something I would frequent on a more regular basis later in my career, when performing exhibit officer duties, I would deal with the forensic evidence a body surrendered up following a serious crime.

My first death report was for a death in custody that occurred a week or so later. The death in question was related to a remand prisoner being held at Tower Bridge Magistrates Court prior to his transfer to prison on a commitment warrant. Accompanied by Inspector Mc, I attended the court where the Gaoler. Sergeant 'Giss' met us. 'Giss's' nickname came from the way he would cadge cigarettes from officers attending the court. He was notorious for always saying to them 'Giss a fag.' I went into the court cell and saw the deceased person someone who had attended court to be dealt with on a non-payment of fine warrant, and as is their right, the magistrates had substituted the fines for something like seven days in custody. The deceased had been taken straight from the court to the cell area where he had been cursorily searched and placed into a cell to await collection by the prison service to serve his sentence. Despite the fact this person was clearly dead, only a qualified doctor can give a professional opinion and certify that to be the case. Clearly, this was not something within my pay grade, so the Force Medical Examiner (FME) was called out to attend and certify life extinct, which he duly did.

Once that was out of the way, I stuck on a set of gloves and checked the person's body for obvious signs of injury, and found nothing untoward. The only item of interest was an empty plastic pills bottle and some loose capsules that were in one of his pockets. These I kept as evidence for the coroner. Once death was certified, the undertakers arrived and took the body away to the mortuary, where a special post mortem was later held that determined the cause of death as being a drugs overdose. No great surprise there. Now a death in custody today, especially one where the person had died from a drugs overdose, would be a major crime investigated by a plethora of different squads. Someone, probably, in this case, the court PC, would be left carrying the can. Luckily, that was not the case at this time.

It was all left to me to deal with, obviously supervised by the relief inspector. I reported it in my notebook, seized exhibits, liaised with the coroner's office, and finally notified the station officer. That was it until a few months later; I went to Southwark Coroners Court, where I gave live evidence to the coroner Sir Montague Levine who ruled accordingly - case complete!

I can tell you that dealing with dead bodies was a lot easier than dealing with their families. I did have to deliver a few death messages, and every time without fail, I was filled with dread from the moment I received the call until I knocked on the door and met the occupant for the first time with the words: "I'm PC Glenister. Can I come in, please? I have some bad news to tell you." Of all the tasks I performed as a police officer, delivering a death message was by far and away the hardest task of all.

---ooo0ooo--

Chapter 18

Pranks

Playing pranks on each other was a way of life that I had no difficulty in participating in. I honestly believe it built character and developed a camaraderie that still exists with my friends and colleagues to this day - a camaraderie very much underpinned by the mantra of 'all for one and one for all.' I knew that if at any time I required assistance, then every available member of the police force would come to my aid to assist - something I likewise would do for them. The police family was not exclusive to officers and very much included the civilian staff who worked alongside us. Many times, an 'urgent assistance' call would be received whilst we were in the station canteen eating or just about to eat our food. Without fail, every officer would immediately leave the canteen and in a stampede down the two flights of stairs into the station yard, jump into the nearest vehicle and race off on the 'blues and twos' to wherever our assistance was needed. We all knew that as soon as we left the canteen on a call like this our food would be collected from the tables by Josie, Flo, Stella, Sylvie or other canteen staff members and kept warm until we returned to eat it. If it was spoilt, then it was thrown away at no extra charge; a fresh one was cooked from scratch that we would eat on our return.

The pranks played were varied, to say the least, with water fights a regular night duty pastime. Pranks continued even when we were off duty. My home at this time was room 66 on the 4th floor at Maurice Drummond Police Section House in Deptford (known affectionately as 'The Drum'). The Drum had a 24-hour attendant service run from an office by the front entrance. It was the attendants who had access to a master key that opened the doors to every room. This 24-hour service meant someone was always there to give an early morning wakeup call for officers working early turn or to ensure they attended court off night duty.

The Drum housed police officers from other stations – for example, Pongo was based at Peckham, whilst Dykesy was based at Tower Bridge. Dykesy and I, though based at the same station, worked a different shift pattern. Both had rooms on the same floor as me. They never stopped playing pranks with their 'piece de resistance' being to enter my name in the night duty attendant wakeup book for a wakeup call on days when I was off at some perverse hour, 4:30 a.m. being a particular favourite. I cannot remember the number of times I was woken up blurry-eyed because of this; something had to be done.

The opportunity for getting even with both 'Pongo' & 'Dykesy' presented itself one day when they both went to work on a late turn. I was off, and that gave me eight hours in which to sort them out. With a few accomplices, I went down to the attendant's office, and using distraction techniques; I liberated the master key from its location in the key cupboard.

My first port of call was 'Dykesy's' room, where every stick of furniture – bed, mattress, chair, cupboard, etc. was removed and taken to the fire exit staircase at the far end of the landing where it was summarily stored one on top of another effectively blocking the fire exit route in the process. Now looking back, this was a pretty stupid thing to do, but at that time, police had Crown immunity from Health & Safety laws, and as getting my own back was my main goal blocking the fire escape staircase was not something that I gave a second thought to. One down and one to go!

'Pongo' was a strapping six-footer who kept a stuffed teddy bear on his bed pillow as a sort of comforter. The Drum at that time was undergoing external works, which had left ropes hanging from the roof down to the ground. Perhaps it was 'Deja Vu," but one of those ropes was hanging pretty much the plumb centre of Pongo's room window. Pongo's teddy bear was the first to suffer as I strangled it with the rope and left it hanging by its neck, clearly visible through the window.

That was followed by a suitably punctured bag of kippers, being strategically hidden under a draw unit. This touch provided a fragrant whiff that lasted for weeks and weeks; so far so good. Now Pongo surprisingly liked steaming hot baths, so for the coup de resistance, gearbox oil was added to his bubble bath toiletries. Apart from his hanging teddy bear, Pongo would be unaware that anything had been tampered with. Satisfied with my work, I returned the master key back to its cupboard, and now all I needed to do now was sit back and wait for the fallout.

'Pongo' was the first to arrive, and as expected, the only thing he noticed out of place was his teddy bear hanging from the rope. I feigned innocence (as you would expect) personally condemning the cowardly, evil person who had committed such a callous crime. I don't think he particularly believed me, but that's life.

'Dykesy," by contrast, had had a busy late turn with lots of prisoners to deal with, so he never got back to his room until after 2:00 a.m. when I was well asleep. He was not a happy bunny when with nothing but sleep on his mind, he opened his bedroom door to find nothing. Not surprisingly, he came straight back to my room and started banging on my door, uttering a few curses and some rather naughty words. I opened the door to find him beside himself. "Daisy, I'm tired, I've had a busy late turn, and I need to sleep. I promise not to play any more pranks on you if you tell me where you have put my furniture." I didn't even try to bluff this one. I felt so sorry for him that I took him to the fire exit stairs and helped him put the furniture back, just so he could get a good night's sleep.

Satisfied, I had repaid them with interest and taught them a lesson they wouldn't forget in a long time. I felt pretty smug with myself as I went back to bed, falling immediately into a well-deserved sleep. It wasn't until the next day that 'Pongo' found out about the doctored toiletries, and that was only after he had poured them into his steaming hot bath. How Pongo could get into the hot water was a mystery. Just running the bath left the room covered in steam; luckily for me, that meant he never got to see the scummy oil lying on the water beneath the bubbles. He soon found out, though when he stepped into the bath, found it was too hot even for him so quickly stood out again, only now he was wearing oily scum 'socks' around his feet and ankles. With cries of 'Daisy' echoing from the bathroom, I figured it was a wise move to go for a walk until he had calmed down.

As for the bag of kippers, after a week or two, the fragrant smell coming from Pongo's' room was drawing complaints from the cleaner and his nearby neighbours. On health grounds, I told Pongo what was causing the smell and where the offending smell was coming from. Playing pranks died down for a month or so, and just when I thought it had stopped completely, I found to my cost that it hadn't.

I was walking towards the Drum from the car park one night when I was soaked through in an unprovoked water ambush in which a water fire extinguisher was emptied onto me from the roof of a first-floor landing. War was declared, and a full-scale water fight broke out. Once the water fight ended, we all showered and changed and went around the corner to the 'Mucky Duck' for a few pints to exchange pleasantries, toasting each other 'until the next time. The Drum management later found during a fire safety inspection that the site's fire extinguishers, for some inexplicable reason, were empty. Strange that!

The Mucky Duck was used by us as a regular meeting place that frequently extended into drinking sessions. It was during one such session that a plan was hatched to play a trick on 'Pongo." Pongo owned a small motorbike that he used to get to and from Peckham on. It was kept in the covered garage area part of the car park immediately behind the 'Drum." The day we chose to play this trick was when Pongo was due to work night duty. Pongo's bike was removed from the covered garage to a secure area, and in its place was a ransom note which said something like 'Information on a lost bike is available from the boys in the Mucky Duck. The cost is a round of drinks.

Sure enough, 30 minutes before he was due to parade, "Pongo' appeared at the Mucky Duck, and despite trying his hardest to get out of buying a drink, it was a case of 'pay up or be late for work." It was no contest, really, so Pongo did the right thing, bought us all a drink each whereupon the motorbike location was provided. Mysteriously and not too sure who did it, the bike had relocated itself into the Drum's ground floor men's toilets, where it was left alongside the urinals.

One prank that didn't go quite as planned happened during night duty. The relief WPCs were the projected targets this night. With precision planning, just prior to the relief returning to the station at midnight for their tea break, a lone ranger went into the ladies toilet on the first floor, lifted the toilet seat, and placed cling film (not too tight) over the pan. The toilet seat was then replaced, and to prevent the handiwork from being discovered, the light bulb was removed. Now the frosted ladies toilet window was visible from the yard area, and you knew when someone opened the ladies toilet door as light from the first-floor landing shone through. It was into this area of the yard that the relief male officers, for some reason, meandered towards to stand and drink their tea whilst staring up at nothingness. The wait was not long before the light appeared at the ladies' toilet window, followed by the sound of a switch being moved up and down. It was not possible to see exactly who it was, so we waited with bated breaths to hear the cries when they started realizing their ablutions were not going in the direction, they thought they would. Well, after all is said and done, "What do you get from surprise pees - clearly wet legs." Unfortunately, our victim this night was none other than Mrs Smith, and it was obvious from her somewhat inelegant outburst that, to say the least, she was not happy. I have never seen the station yard clear so fast. There were cars and people running off in all directions as she complained to the station officer, who had the task of pouring oil over troubled waters. Luckily, that cost the relief a few rounds of drinks, but nothing more was said about it.

Ghurkha was the victim of a prank that saw him dragging a dead cat along behind his Morris Marina Coupe. A dead cat was found – it never needed a vet to pronounce life extinct – that was clear from the tire tracks that stretched right across its body so that it was more like a rug than a cat. I guess it had been flattened by a large dray lorry as it was in a gutter in Shad Thames. The dead cat was as stiff as a board and splayed out in the shape of a flying squirrel. It was collected, and a length of rope was used to tie it to the rear bumper of Ghurkha's car - not quite a 'Puss in boot' and more a 'Puss outside the boot." Hopefully, it would fly like a kite once Ghurkha drove off. Now it was a waiting game until we finished night duty and left for home. Ghurkha was the first to drive off along Tooley Street, where like a relief convoy, he was followed by Mike 2 and a line of cars. The flattened cat didn't fly like a kite as we hoped it would, although it did bump along with Ghurkha as he sped away. It was not long before Ghurkha realized something was amiss, so he stopped in Jamaica Road, which is where we all overtook him, laughing at him as we did so. Ghurkha took it in good fun. He removed his furry companion and deposited it in a roadside waste bin.

Pranks continued throughout my probation and onto the various squads I was fortunate enough to work on. The one rule was that if you played pranks on others, you had to be able to take pranks played on you – very much a case of 'give and take." If you can't take – don't give

---ooo0ooo--

Chapter 19

Acceptance

I had been on the relief for about six months when there was a vacancy for someone to make a foursome in the card school. I just happened to be in the canteen at the time sitting in my non-card school designated seat when the duty officer Inspector Mc called me over.

'Daisy, how are you at cards?' said Inspector Mc

'Okay," I replied.

'Good; sit down. You're in the card school."

The game being played was affectionately known as 'Hunt the lady," although it was not always referred to by this name. Played over five hands, the winner won the princely sum of 10p from each player. It was during this game that I realized my literacy skills were far from up to speed. It happened when the game was into the last two hands.

Inspector Mc happened to mention, "So, this is the penultimate hand."

I replied, "No sir, I believe there's another hand after this one.

The raucous laughter from the other players, together with universal shouts of "you plonker," made me realize that

I needed to improve upon my understanding of words. My lack of literacy was costing me money as the card school fined me teas all around for being a dullard. In the circumstances, a small price to pay. That said, being accepted into the relief card school was a signally high honour for, in effect, it meant I was not now being treated as a liability, more as an equal with other relief members.

This may have been the first time I was called a plonker, but it surely was not the last time. In fact, plonker was a compliment compared with some of the more insulting words I have been called over the years?

One particular occasion when I was to be the subject of name-calling happened shortly after I paraded one day for the early turn shift. A teleprinter message had been sent to all stations to raise the Union Jack flag to celebrate some particular event – what the event was, I can no longer remember. Either way, my briefing sergeant said, "Daisy, after the parade, collect the union jack flag from the station officer, get onto the roof and raise it on the flag pole."

"Sure thing, serge," I replied, and once the parade was over, I went and collected the Union Jack flag, trudged up to the top floor of the station building, and climbed out through a roof access window to proudly stand in front of the station's flag pole. I connected the flag toggles into the flag pole guide rope and then started pulling the ropes until the flag unfurled and could not be raised any further. That's when I tied the guidelines off on a rope cleat - job done, and off I went out on foot patrol.

I was blissfully unaware that anything was amiss until Botty, the station reserve, called me up on the radio saying '293 – receiving."

"Mike Tango - Go ahead."

"293, is there any reason why you have put the flag up the wrong way so that it is now flying at half-mast? I've just had three telephone calls from the public asking me which member of the Royal family has passed away.

I returned as fast as I could, and sure enough, the flag was upside down and flying at half-mast. If I wasn't red-faced already, I certainly was by the time I climbed the stairs in double quick time, back onto the roof to lower, change and then raise the flag correctly. How was I supposed to know that a flag has a top and bottom – that didn't stop my fellow relief members, those that were not in fits of laughter, from calling me various names using language that was a lot stronger than plonker.

Still, life is one big learning curve, and that's one mistake I won't repeat, especially as I vowed, I would never raise a flag again no matter who asked me.

---ooo0ooo--

Chapter 20

Beat Crimes

The Beat Crimes' office at Tower Bridge Police station was run from a small 1st-floor office by a PC called Arthur. The beat crimes office was virtually the piggy in the middle that separated the ladies toilet on one side and the CID office on the other. Unlike today where the CRIS machine is king, back then, Arthur managed a paper system on his lonesome, making all the follow-up inquiries, circulating stolen property, and compiling reports. The only time that a relief PC was allocated a crime to investigate was when a suspect became known and needed to be arrested.

In many ways, the two-year police officer probation was akin to completing a modern-day NVQ apprenticeship. I had to evidence everything I did, and if I didn't pass all the exams, it was a good night to you and you were gone. One big difference was there was no qualification when you successfully completed the 'School of Hard Knocks' and the 'University of Life' courses. We did, though, celebrate graduation with fellow alumni in a bar for a drink or two, or three….

My probationer police officer status meant I could report crimes, but I was not permitted to investigate crimes until I had completed a one-week 'Beat Crimes Investigators' course. This I did sometime around July 1977, and virtually on my return from the course, Arthur collared me and said something to the effect.

"Daisy, I've got a simple crime with a named suspect that I'm going to allocate to you. It's a piece of cake; all you need to do is contact the victim, take a statement and then arrange for her to attend the magistrate's court. Just have her present with you when you make an application for an arrest warrant. It's dead simple."

"Thanks, Arthur, I appreciate that," I said as I took details off the crime sheet and signed my very first beat crime as an investigating officer. This would be a good crime arrest for me to write in my probationer arrest book. I could smell that 'collar' a mile away, even though he never knew what was about to descend on him.

So as Arthur said, the matter was pretty simple. The victim 'Mrs A' alleged her estranged husband 'Mr A' entered her house and stole money from a front room sideboard. The money had been collected from her friends to pay an outstanding catalogue debt. When he left the house, he took that money with him.

I thought back to the definition of theft:

No problem, all the points for theft are proved – money belonging to another, dishonestly appropriated with intention to permanently deprive – Simples. Next, I took a witness statement and arranged a suitable date for my witness to be present at the magistrate's court when I made an application for an arrest warrant. So, together with a signed witness statement, my signed information and the witness, I arrived at Tower Bridge magistrate's court just as it opened, which is when I arranged with the Court 1 warrant officer to put me to the front of the morning's list with a quick warrant application. Court 1 at Tower Bridge Magistrates had a public seating area at the back of it made up of two rows of benches – one in front of the other for court attendees to sit and wait for their case to be called. A separate seating area was provided for members of the legal profession, social workers and the police. It was sod's law that on this particular day, the courtroom was packed to the gunnels. "Court Rise," cried the court officer as Cookie, the

102

magistrate, entered, and everyone dutifully stood as Cookie walked in and sat down. I went into the witness box when the court officer called officer for application.

Cookie said, "Yes, officer."

I said, "Application for an arrest warrant, sir," and handed over my signed information and a copy of the witness statement to the court usher to pass over to Cookie. As she did so I added, "The witness is in court."

Up until then, I thought this was a walk in the park, a breeze. Now, normally getting a warrant was a simple matter of swearing information on oath, after which the warrant was granted. That did not happen this time. Cookie had a look at my paperwork and brought me back down to Earth with a thump when he went into a lecture that went something like this:

"Officer, officer, officer…oh why, oh why, oh why did you not come and speak to me about this privately in my chambers?" With all eyes in the court now firmly focused on me, they watched as I was publicly berated by Cookie while we went on. "This is a husband-and-wife matter, and you know that under section 30 subsection 4 of the Theft Act 1968, spouses cannot steal from each other except in certain circumstances. These circumstances do not appear to apply in this case. Application denied."

With a flea in my ear, Cookie handed me back my paperwork and summarily sent me on my way. My witness even felt sorry for me, although probably not as sorry as I felt at that time. I don't recall being told about Section 30 Subsection 4 at Hendon, so, on leaving the court, I went and found out pretty damn quick. Cookie had been spot-on; Section 30 Subsection 4 did indeed state spouses cannot steal from each other, except in certain situations—a minor setback certainly but not the end of the line.

One thing I had learnt as a police officer was to look for other options in the face of adversity, so I overcame section 30 (4) by changing the victim from that of the wife to that of the mail-order company. My next application was successful, and in the fullness of time, Mr A was lifted and dealt with for theft.

There is nothing like experiential learning to improve knowledge and test your ability to change situations to your advantage and learning was provided free—all thanks to Cookie.

---ooo0ooo--

Chapter 21

Up a Tree Without a Paddle

Things happen quickly when you least expect it, and it did just that for Ghurkha and me on night duty when we were sent out on foot patrol in Tower Bridge Road. There we were discussing the meaning of life when a call from Beardy came over our personal radio. Beardy and Vulch were about to stop two males they had seen acting suspiciously in the Abbey Street area, and he wanted nearby units to make their way to back them up when they were stopped. Ghurkha and I were literally just around the corner, so we made our way post-haste to join them, arriving in time to assist them to stop these two individuals: one was a person called Fitzalbert Williams, and the other male with him had the surname of Donovan. Vulch started searching Donovan and found a large six or seven-inch Bowie type knife secreted in the top of his belt along the small of his back. Vulch seized the knife, arrested Donovan for possessing an offensive weapon and took him to a police car where they sat in the rear. Donovan's free time had just been cancelled. Despite his loss of freedom he was being totally compliant with Vulch and our services as far as he was concerned were not required.

Fitzalbert Williams, on the other hand, had other ideas. As soon as Donovan was seated in the back seat of the police car, Williams produced a gun from somewhere and started bringing it to aim position uttering threats of violence as he did so. It was lucky for us that Beardy reacted quicker, somehow managing to knock the gun sideways from Williams's grasp, causing it to fall from his hand onto the footpath immediately followed by Beardy, who fell spread-eagle on the floor with his body now covering Williams's gun. So, with Vulch and Beardy, both otherwise engaged, Williams took the opportunity to have it away on his toes along Abbey Street, closely followed by Ghurkha and I. Williams turned left off Abbey Street, going into a number of small roads before eventually turning right into an estate road where I caught up with him and brought him to the ground, which is where Ghurkha joined in, and collectively, we restrained Williams in arm locks.

At that time, handcuffs were not standard police personal issues. Handcuffs were only for use in exceptional cases, and even then, prisoners secured in this way were not allowed to be seen handcuffed in public. Handcuffs would not become police standard-issue until sometime in the future. With no handcuffs available, Williams's hands remained free. Whilst awaiting police transport, Williams was securely restrained up against a wall. In this position, he did not pose a threat. Our transport this night was a three-door Allegro panda car driven by Blind Pugh. It was not an ideal transport, but with no other transport en route; it was that or nothing.

The car was really snug for the back seat passengers with yours truly seated behind the driver, Williams in the middle and Ghurkha sat to his left, leaving the front passenger seat empty. Blind Pugh started to drive out of the service road and right into Fendall Street when Williams, who up until then had been somewhat subdued, started to have other ideas. During the journey William's managed to pull both hands free, placing them onto Blind Pugh's shoulders and violently yanking him backwards in his seat. This caused him to release his grip on the steering wheel and lose control of the vehicle. Within the space of a second or two the car swerved violently across the road, mounted the kerb and started to climb up the trunk of a roadside tree. The headlights were now pointed skywards apparently looking for alien aircraft. We eventually came to rest with our two rear wheels on the ground and our two front wheels grasping at air. It reminded me a bit of a 'Hi Ho Silver' moment. Now with 'tree' persons - sorry, should be 'three' persons - in the back, the only avenue of escape for Williams lay through the empty front passenger seat.

The problem for Williams was that somehow, he had to get from the back seat into the empty front seat and open the passenger door to have any chance of escaping, something he would have to do whilst being assailed from each side by Ghurkha and me. What was in Williams's favour was the way we were so tightly packed together as it made freedom of movement difficult. Clearly, Ghurkha sat on Williams left posed the most immediate threat to him, making it into the front passenger seat, and literally seconds after he had made us crash, he attacked Ghurkha, poking both his thumbs into Ghurkha's eye sockets trying to blind him. Williams stuck them in as far as he could, wiggling them about as he did so.

Ghurkha understandably was screaming in pain and not really in any position to stop Williams as he edged slowly from the back seat over to the empty front seat. With Blind Pugh temporarily out of the game, it left Moi, the 'lone ranger,' to take emergency action. Hitting Williams to the side of his face as hard as I could a fair few times made him reconsider his attack on Ghurkha, whereby he removed his thumbs from Ghurkha's eyes to concentrate solely on me. That was the right result for Ghurkha as otherwise he could well have been blinded or lost an eye. So now, it was a war of attrition between Williams and me, and one he was sorely losing. He was persistent, though, as he continued to edge nearer the passenger door, groping about for the handle, presumably looking to open it. Unfortunately for Williams, I was mirroring what he was doing effectively, lying like a dead weight on top of him and hitting him at every opportunity in the process; slowly, he pulled both of us towards the door, but progress was pitifully slow.

I was now being carried along by Williams, as he moved so I moved, which made it easier for me to move my hands about. So, I decided to rack up the volume and hope very soon for Williams to 'Make my Day' as I steadily removed my truncheon from a trouser pocket, praying for sufficient clearance to hit him right over the Swede. With everything happening fast, it was what I would describe as being a bit disjointed and fuzzy, and when I saw the car door begin to open, I immediately thought Williams had managed to open it and was about to escape. No, no, that won't do at all. So, in a blur, I struck a blow with my truncheon at Williams's head. Unbeknownst to me, it was Beardy who had opened the door to help me, and it was him that I unfortunately hit. Luckily what with the limited space in which to strike I only managed to catch him a glancing blow to the side of his head when he got in the way of my truncheon. As help began to arrive, Williams had played all his cards, and the game was now well and truly over. This time Williams was stuck face down in a van and most definitely suitably restrained before being taken to Tower Bridge Police Station to join his buddy Donovan in the charge room.

Both were interviewed. As for Donovan, he distanced himself from Williams as soon as he could. Yes, he had been found with a knife, but that was it. It would have been difficult for Donovan to explain the Bowie knife as a toothpick, and he was charged with possession of an offensive weapon and sent in custody to Tower Bridge Magistrates the next day, where he pleaded guilty at the earliest opportunity and was sentenced accordingly.

At the station, the gun was found to be an imitation, although, to all intents and purposes, it could easily have passed for the real thing. Ghurkha was off work for a few weeks but thankfully suffered no permanent eye damage.

Man fought police like 'a wild animal'

FITZALBERT WILLIAMS, said to have fought three policemen "like a wild animal" and to have caused their panda car to crash, was jailed for four years at the Old Bailey this week.

Williams (20), of 83 Ondine-rd., Peckham, threatened to kill two police officers after they found him with a gun in Abbey-st., Bermondsey. The weapon, later found to be a starting pistol, was knocked out of his hand by one officer, it was said.

He kneed one policeman in the groin trying to escape, later fought three officers in the panda car, which crashed when Williams tried to strangle the driver, the jury heard.

He was cleared of assault causing actual bodily harm to PC Stephen Brown, but found guilty of attempting to cause him grievous bodily harm. During the fight in the car he had tried to gouge out the officer's eye, said counsel.

He was cleared of causing actual bodily harm to the driver, PC Anthony Sampson, but convicted of assaulting him to resist arrest. And he was cleared of stealing or receiving the pistol but found guilty of damaging the police car and using the pistol to resist arrest.

Sentencing him, the judge said, "You fought like a wild animal. You unleashed what can only be described as a furious assault on PC Brown."

Williams had attacked the officers a few weeks after being released from a sentence for assault on police.

It was probably "panic" and fear of returning to jail, that prompted him to lose control, said defence counsel.

Williams was charged with various offences and remanded in custody until his trial at the Central Criminal Court Old Bailey. He was found guilty on a number of counts and was sentenced to a term of four years imprisonment. The court case made the local rag, although which one I can no longer remember.

It was reported that Williams's defense counsel in mitigation stated: "He had only just been released from prison for an assault on police, and it was probably panic and fear of returning to jail that prompted him to lose control." Great excuse, although I am not quite sure how that explains why he and Donovan were both away from their homes, late at night carrying weapons. Quite probably, they were looking to commit a robbery or similar crime, something their arrests prevented from happening. Perhaps it was the catalyst that led to change, but shortly after this, police officers were issued with handcuffs kept in a discreet belt case, carried out of sight lest it upset the public - a completely different mindset from today's officers who wear Kwik cuffs, CS spray, and body armour openly on display. That's 'change' for you.

---ooo0ooo---

Chapter 22

Domestic Violence

It is not possible to recite every incident my colleagues and I were called upon to deal with during this initial posting other than to say it was a lot. There were some calls, though, that stood out. The first was Daniel D. Daniel D was a bully and a wife beater; he stood about 5'9" tall with a short, stocky wiry type of build. It is difficult to understand why but he was married to a charming pretty lady who put up with the violent behaviour he subjected her to on pretty much a daily basis. It was the result of a disturbance call to Daniel D's home address on the Cooper Astley Estate that, along with JT, I responded to.

Arriving at the front door, we knocked on it a few times before it was opened by Daniel D's wife, displaying clearly the imprint of a fresh bite mark on the top of her left breast. The hurt and pain that must have caused her were off the scale of violence. Appearing behind her was her husband, Daniel D, with a thin line of blood around his mouth. I was not a great fan of his to start with, but right now, I detested him with a vengeance and felt my blood boil at what I suspected he had done. In his normal belligerent manner, Daniel D said to his wife, "I told you not to open the door." Then turning to us, he said, "You lot can F-- off" and attempted to shut the door in our face – not a good move. JT stuck his foot in the door frame and, ignoring Daniel D, spoke directly to the wife.

'Who did that to you?' pointing to the bite mark. We pretty much knew the answer before it was given. She was too frightened to answer that but luckily: Daniel D said, "I did; now you know you can F--- off."

JT: "You're under arrest for assault."

Daniel D: "Who by? You and who else's army?"

That pretty much signalled that the art of conversation had irretrievably broken down. It was no contest as we dragged this obnoxious, odious little man bodily out of his front door, threw him straight into the wall opposite, hitting it with sufficient force to knock the wind out of his sails, and suffer other injuries in the process. That was followed by JT saying, "Like I said, you're under arrest," and we unceremoniously dragged him down the stairwell of the block to the ground floor, where we shoved him face-down into the footwell of the station van and took him to the police station. It's funny how many things there are in stairwells to bump into certainly when you are not being too discerning about negotiating them safely.

Daniel was banged up in a cell, charged with assault and remanded in custody to court. I do not know what happened to him, although, interestingly, after we had pointed out the errors of his ways, and the court had finished with him, we never got another disturbance call to that house. Perhaps Daniel had learnt a valuable lesson, namely, there's always someone bigger swimming in the great pool of life who can repay bad manners with interest.

On another occasion, Botty, the relief reserve officer, dealt with a domestic disturbance. Now, for the record, Botty was an ex-serviceman who had been through the mill. He had more lives than a cat, knew more tricks than Houdini, and was not a man to be taken lightly. You upset him at your peril. To give you an example of how he dealt with issues, I was present one day in the reserve room when he took a call from an obviously irate person. All I heard was half the conversation, but it finished with something like "Oh really. Do you know who I am? No. Then go F--- yourself,' followed by him slamming the phone down. I said to Botty, "What was that about?"

He replied, "Some wanker calling himself a DAC was having a go at me for not answering the phone quick enough. Well, now he will have to phone back and guess what? I'm going to the canteen," and off he trotted, repeating his terms of endearment about a senior officer. It was not too long after that that the station officer received a phone call from a DAC affectionately known as Crazy Horse, who ranted and raved to him about the way he had just been spoken to on the phone. When the station officer asked the name of the person he had spoken to, Crazy Horse was not able to supply it, and there, the complaint stopped.

Anyway, I digress. On this night duty, Botty had been given a day pass from the reserve room and posted to ride shotgun with the duty officer as they drove around the manor. As normally happens when you are minding your own business, they happened across a distraught lady running along the Old Kent Road. Naturally, with them being knights in shining armour, they stopped and spoke to her to find out what the problem was: no great mystery there; it was her husband. The woman was clearly upset and told them both to leave her alone because if her husband caught her talking to them, it would end in a fight, and they might get hurt. Lo and behold, her husband, a largish man, suddenly appeared on the scene carrying a dog lead in his right hand. Strange that as there was no dog with him, I guess the lead was intended to be used as some sort of offensive weapon.

Despite the fact that the police were present, the husband started swinging the dog lead about his head, apparently looking to lay it on his wife, which is when Botty intervened. Botty said, "Put the dog lead down." The husband did not comply and continued to swing the lead above his head, so Botty raised his arm above his head and snagged the dog lead around his tunic sleeve a couple of times, which allowed

Botty to pull the husband towards him into what is known as the intimate zone. Once there, Botty grabbed hold of the hand, holding the lead and twisted the husband's fingers backwards in one fluid movement. Now in control, Botty told him in no uncertain terms to 'put the lead' down. The husband's reply of 'You'll have to break my fingers to get the leadoff me' was not a clever thing to say in the circumstances. Fast forward a minute. Botty now had possession of the lead, whilst the husband was nursing two rather sore fingers, that broken or not would need to be strapped for a couple of weeks to heal. The learning curve here was for the husband to take a break from being a stupid jerk every now and again, something that Botty had helped him accomplish.

Now it's a funny thing with husband-and-wife disputes; one minute they hate each other, and the next thing, their headlong in love again. That was exactly what happened on this occasion where once the woman's husband had been put in his place, the wife leapt to her husband's defence, crying, "Don't hurt him, don't hurt him. Well, it was too late for that, and so, it was that they left the woman to care for her husband in a role reversal that saw the husband now suffering from extremely sore fingers that would need strapping together and take a few weeks to heal properly, with the wife now in control. Hopefully, the pain and suffering would last long enough for him to reflect on his poor behaviour. Problem solved – family reunited, no more cause for police action. Botty and the duty officer drove off into the night for a well-earned cup of tea.

When violence erupts around you, it is not always directed at you. This was something that happened to me one-night duty when I stopped a speeding car in Great Dover Street. The car contained five males, the driver, a front-seat passenger and three rear-seat passengers. I was on my lonesome at the time, so I asked for backup, and Ghurkha made his way over to me in Panda 1. Whilst waiting for Ghurkha to appear, I walked over to the vehicle and spoke to the driver about his speeding. It was during this conversation that I caught a faint smell of intoxicating liquor. Being stone-cold sober, it clearly wasn't emanating from me. The driver was not unpleasant as I pointed out he was speeding. That's when I asked him his name, which is when the middle of the three males in the back, who I will call Gobby, decided to pipe up with the words 'Don't tell the little Hitler anything. You've done nothing wrong.'

Now, if that wasn't bad enough, Gobby didn't leave it there going on and on giving it some, despite the fact that his two companions sitting on either side of him were telling him to shut up. Well, enough is enough; now it was time to get my own back, so taking the car keys from the driver, I said to him, "I suspect you have been drinking, and I require you to take a breath test.' I knew Ghurkha was on his way, so I told him he would have to wait a short while until the kit arrived. Like I said, the driver was no problem whatsoever, but the four other passengers then decided to get out of the car, clearly intent on trying to sort the problem out. I relayed this on my radio to Ghurkha, who was nearby and closing fast. The situation was looking a bit bleak, and it wasn't looking too good for me, so I considered my options:

1. Take my uniform off, mingle with the crowd and walk away – not in these circumstances.
2. Run – not an option either since they were all fitter than me
3. Threaten them with my wooden truncheon - laughable
4. Speak to them and hope they would listen

Thankfully I never had to make a decision as 'Gobby' was now about to get his comeuppance because Gobby's three fellow passengers all turned on him and started to meet out their own form of discipline to let them know they were not very happy. Clearly, as I was dealing with the driver, I, unfortunately, didn't see how he got the bloody nose and a black eye – injuries usually associated with falling over. I might have even had to help 'Gobby' with a bit of first aid, but luckily, the noise of Ghurkha's squealing wheels as he came around the Bricklayers Arms roundabout made everyone apart from Gobby stop what they were doing and turn towards the source. 'Gobby' was now face down on the floor to all intents and purposes forgotten about, which is where he remained for a minute or two. It's funny that 'Gobby' was not so 'Gobby' after being disciplined. That said, it was he who had upset me and forced my hand, and now the final act was about to be played as the driver blew a positive breath test and was arrested. That meant the vehicle was locked up and left in the street, leaving the four passengers to make their own way home on foot. As I drove away, I left them still arguing in Great Dover Street, secretly hoping that 'Gobby' was going to be made to suffer a bit more for his poor behaviour.

Summary justice – a much-maligned practise that on this occasion provided someone with a lesson in humility that they will hopefully take on board

---ooo0ooo---

Chapter 23

Mental Health

Dealing with people suffering from mental health problems was not something I particularly relished - in part because there was always an uncertainty as to how they would react because the person you are trying to help did not necessarily know that to be the case. It was always a judgment call as to what actions had to be taken, by force, if need be, but as sympathetically as possible to reduce the need for causing undue stress. I had been told that people who suffer mental illness are often capable of feats of strength that defy belief, and it was not something I wanted to test at first hand, so using force was definitely the last option in my armoury to consider. Mental disorder by its very nature could mean that a suffering person was not in control of all their faculties, in which case the only recourse the police had was to take them to a place of safety, e.g., a police station where a duty officer could have them detained for 36 hours in order to have them assessed by suitably qualified staff. In practice, this meant they would be taken straight to a hospital for assessment and treatment.

The first mental illness call I attended was in response to a telephone call made by an elderly mother for help. The caller stated that her son was diagnosed with a severe mental disorder that was controlled by medication. The son, for some reason, had not taken the medication as required and was now sitting in a chair in her front room staring fixedly at the television holding a glass in a shaking hand. Not a good sign! So, mob-handed, we turned up at the mothers flat wearing gloves, thick clothing and a pair of handcuffs just in case.

On arrival, the mother opened the front door to us, and we entered the front room where her son was indeed sat in an armchair staring straight at the wall, holding in his shaking right hand an empty ½ pint glass by the stem. I had learnt the hard way that glass was something to be very wary of, especially in these circumstances when it could suddenly become a weapon or projectile. As one of my colleagues spoke softly to him, I very slowly inched my way towards him, albeit with beads of sweat rolling down my face, until the opportunity to get close enough to grab the glass from his hand presented itself, allowing me to move it out of harm's way. After the glass had been removed, we entered into a clipped conversation with the man, where we managed to get him to take the medication he required. We waited until the medication had kicked in, and he started to behave 'normally' again and then left. Job done!

The second call was received from nurses at St. Olave's Hospital looking after potentially violent patients at a secure mental health ward. This time it was the nurses who had failed to give the patient his intravenous medication in time, and knowing the patient's history, the nurses feared for their own safety. Again, the whole of the night duty relief – yes, all six of us - turned up at the ward where we found about eight male nurses all huddled together whispering giving off the vibes that this was not going to be a walk in the park, the patient according to them was potentially ultra-violent. The potential problem for my fellow officers and me in particular to consider was that we could all get assaulted, maybe hospitalised by this patient, who would not be culpable for any injuries he inflicted - so we were on a hiding to nothing - damned if we do and damned if we don't.

We had a quick conference, and a bit like the scene from 'One flew over the Cuckoo's Nest – along with the nurse's, we entered the secure ward and armed with a loaded hypodermic syringe, we went to confront this behemoth. The picture painted of the patient by the nurses was nothing like what we found. Our behemoth was lying on his bed, completely unfazed by our presence, and again we spoke softly to him as we carefully took hold of a limb each and held it down whilst a nurse stuck the needle in his backside. Behemoth or not, he never made a murmur, which just goes to show you can never tell, as he was more like a mouse than a lion, at least it was on this occasion.

---ooo0ooo---

Chapter 24

Neighbour Disputes

Neighbour disputes are a constant source of aggravation that can escalate to unprecedented levels of violence. From the police's viewpoint, getting a win-win situation between all parties as soon as possible reduces the likelihood of getting a repeat call back. Most times, it works, but sometimes it doesn't. One night duty, I was out on patrol with Inspector Mc when we took a call to a disturbance at the local Chinese take away in Tower Bridge Road. When we turned up, the place was as quiet as a grave, and absolutely no sign of disturbance did we note. I suppose having a one-sided conversation with a Chinese speaking owner didn't help with getting to the bottom of the problem, especially as his knowledge of English was limited to two words – namely, "flied lice," which didn't help us very much, so we turned to leave.

That was when a white male well known to us by the name of Billy was suddenly produced by the Chinese owner's staff from the back kitchen area. I say produced because Billy was tied up in chicken wire that went around and around his body, meaning at best, he was only capable of waddling in duck-like steps. Not only had Billy been tied up, but it was also clear that he had been systematically subjected to a severe beating that had left him red, black and blue. Now Billy, along with his band of friends, was a local pain in the backside and was considered one of our frequent visitors who pretty much held a day ticket to visit the police station charge room as often as he liked.

Inspector Mc said, "Can you speak Chinese, Daisy."

I said, "Apart from ordering from a menu, NO."

I started to think back to my training. *Now which scenario covered this at Hendon? Err none. Oh dear…still, there were a couple of options open.*

1. Arrest everyone and shut the shop. Doing that would probably have caused a riot with the locals waiting patiently for their food.

2. Take the shop owner to the station and find out from him what had happened. That would take ages and need an interpreter.

3. Take Billy Boy to the station, have him seen by the police doctor and find out from him what had happened, no interpreter needed for that.

4. Walk away and leave Billy boy there and pretend we hadn't seen him; my choice but not legal.

Inspector Mc chose option three, and with Billy still wrapped in chicken wire, we placed him into our car and took him to the station.

So, what had Billy boy done that deserved this treatment? Well, Billy and his friends had gone into the takeaway and ordered food from the menu. They waited for it to arrive and decided it would be funny to grab the food from the counter and run away without paying for it - clearly not a good decision, because Billy boy was too slow, and as his friends made good their escape, he got captured. That's when his luck changed because he was taken back to the takeaway shop and through to a backroom area where he was trussed up in chicken wire and subjected to a form of chop suey that was not shown as an item on the shop menu. The end result in the cold light of day meant that Billy and his friends could all be arrested for theft, and staff members in the Chinese takeaway could be arrested with assault. Now for police to do that, they needed witnesses, but as Billy and the takeaway shop owner both refused to supply witness statements, it was dealt with as a civil dispute where names and addresses were exchanged. This was not quite a win-win situation, though, as a few months later, a second incident occurred at the takeaway that resulted in the death of a Chinese youth for which Billy and one of his friends later stood trial and copped porridge pudding.

On another occasion that occurred shortly after Inspector Mc had left and our new duty officer Torchy had arrived, we took a call to a disturbance between eight females at a block of flats in Cluny Place just off of Tower Bridge Road. Sure enough, on arrival, I could see eight women on the fourth-floor landing giving it large about something or other.

We both went up the stairs to the fourth-floor balcony –
never could understand why disturbances always take place
high up. "Hello ladies, what's the problem?" A good
assumption made as I noticed that at least four of them were
holding bottles, lumps of wood and bricks. Now, of these
eight ladies, seven were rather well proportioned, whilst the
eighth was an attractive looking petite lady some might even
say very fit.

Both sides were evenly matched - four apiece. This
number fell by half after the possibility of arrest was thrown
into the mix. They promptly left the scene leaving only the
fit woman and three others to worry about. These four
though were still at opposite ends of the 'let's be nice to each
other' spectrum. Clearly, criminal charges could have been
brought, for example, threatening behaviour and possession
of an offensive weapon, but this dispute needed to be nipped
in the bud, so a van was summonsed, and all four were
arrested for causing a 'breach of the peace.' When the van
arrived, three ladies walked into the van, and one decided
not to. I'll leave it to your imagination as to who that one
was, but it took four officers, each holding an arm and leg
apiece, to place that fourth member into the van without
causing too much damage to her pride and dignity. The end
result was a night in the cells for all of them followed by an
appearance at the Magistrates Court, where they were all
bound over to keep the peace.

Now it's funny what a night in the cells does to a person for whatever it was they had been upset about the day before; when they left the court after being bound over, they left it together crossing Tooley Street into Tower Bridge Road talking to each other as if they were best of friends.

Job done – Oh, in case you are wondering, it was the fit one that didn't want to go for a ride with us.

---ooo0ooo---

Chapter 25

Road Blocks

Roadblocks were held pretty much at least once during every night duty. That's when the whole relief would work together to stop every vehicle in a specific location. With all roads leading to a bottleneck covered by uniformed beat officers supported by a strategically placed wireless car, all vehicles had to stop at the roadblock or be chased and stopped. At the time, we cited Section 66 Metropolitan Police Act as the power to stop and search. As we went about our work, no one ever challenged us about the reason why they had been stopped. Roadblocks were an effective way to detect crime, and would generally lead to a number of arrests for offences that included being wanted on warrant, drink driving, driving whilst disqualified, theft as well as reporting people for various road traffic offences. It was whilst manning one of these roadblocks that I happened to stop a single male driver in a vehicle that could best be described as a heap.

I asked him his name, and he failed the initiative test by giving me some pony personal details, which went something like - Dickie Bird, Nest cottage, Treetops, Acorn Grove in Oak. Needless to say, he won the booby prize to take a short all-inclusive paid break in a fully furnished studio flat complete with a concierge at the five-star Tower Bridge Station Hotel.

Dickie Bird, it turned out, had trotted out of the family home following a feisty argument a few months before. To all intents and purposes, he had vanished off the face of the Earth and had been living rough in his very own mobile home – his car. The smell coming from within the car from the discarded food packages, clothing and stained underwear told its own story – It was certainly not a chariot to carry a fair maiden off in. A few months without money meant Dickie had resorted to dishonesty in order to eat. Now was payback time. Investigating what he had done was not something that could be done overnight, and so he was entered into the person at the station register (book 12) and binned up in his cell pending initial interview.

At this time, authorisation to detain him for up to 72 hours could be given by the Commander, and funnily enough, that's exactly how long it took for the matter to be fully investigated. Whilst he was in custody, I arranged for his father to attend and speak to Dickie Bird so that hopefully they could put aside their differences and makeup. Enquiries complete, Dickie was charged with a range of theft and driving offences and sent in custody to court the next day when he copped a plea. Dickie's father spoke up for him in the court, which must have had some impact on the stipendiary magistrates because instead of giving him porridge, he sentenced him to probation, meaning he could leave the court that same day. Now a lot smarter and definitely not as smelly, and now reunited with his father he took time out to thank me for arresting him as he left the court. Hopefully, this episode had brought him back to reality, turned his life around made him hell-bent on getting back onto the straight and narrow. I was feeling really positive about Dickie's future, which is more than I could say for the next pair of duffers.

The two duffers in question, Mr. A and Mr. B, were arrested during the afternoon whilst working a late turn shift for stealing lead and other metals from a number of derelict houses in the Abbeyfield Road SE16 area. Caught red-handed, they were taken back to Tower Bridge, where they were searched, and their property bagged up before they were placed into the cells to await charges. A police national computer (PNC) check revealed both were well-known thieves, who, as it happened, were both disqualified drivers. Now, as neither of them was a local who lived in the area, the question arose as to how they would carry a couple of hundredweight of scrap metal to the scrapyard to sell – perhaps they had a car parked nearby, and sure enough when we re-examined their personal property what should we find but a single car key. Game on.

Whilst other officers dealt with Mr A & Mr B; I went to the area in which they had been arrested and started searching for a likely car. It was lucky I was in uniform as I could well have been arrested for 'Sus' with the number of cars I tried the key in. My perseverance paid off when the key opened a Ford or Vauxhall saloon that could be theirs. It was difficult to know for sure because most of the cars parked around there were of a similar ilk – at the lower end of the car spectrum.

Either way, it was a fair -to -middling chance it was theirs, so now it was all dependent upon whether they went to that car. If that were the case then a roadblock was planned to start just around the corner from it that they would have no option but drive straight into – if it went as planned for sure, one of them would get nicked again. We hurried back to the station to break the good news to the relief, who went about quickly charging and bailing them from the station. That's when the real fun started as with police officers placed at strategic locations; we followed our prey as they trudged along Jamaica Road, inexorably making their way back to where they had been arrested a few hours earlier. With them both being watched every step of the way, we were all able to keep well clear and make our way to the roadblock positions we had chosen an hour or so earlier. There we waited patiently until bingo, they both got into the car, and with Mr A driving, they drove off around the corner to find a roadblock manned by the same police that had just bailed them from Tower Bridge Police Station.

No need to go down the path of 'Is this your car? Mr A was immediately arrested for driving whilst disqualified and taken back to Tower Bridge Police Station. It was a win double for us, for we knew that either way, one was coming with us. As for Mr B, we left him in the street, facing up to a long walk home. Mr A perhaps was the lucky one as he got a lift to the station, where he was fed and watered before being given a bed for the night. Both Mr A and Mr B were lost causes, really, career criminals through and through who were beyond salvation by a mere police constable. Mind you; I helped to control their disqualified driving. I had the car removed to the police car pound where it was later sent off for destruction. One less car on the roads to worry about. Nasty or what – Who said the police weren't game for a laugh.

---ooo0ooo---

Chapter 26

Demonstrations

Being sent on aid to police various demonstrations and events was a way of life; pretty much a weekly basis. The drain on police officers, especially with the larger demonstrations, could only be achieved by cancelling all rest days and extending the early turn and night duty relief hours from 8 to 12 hours tours. This released the late turn relief, which meant you potentially had half of London's police force engaged in demonstration duties at any one time.

It was extremely debilitating for police officers to work continuously at this level for any length of time, and thankfully large-scale commitments such as the Notting Hill Carnival were relatively few and far between. Tiredness, therefore, was a big issue for all officers, whether on aid or working at the station, to contend with following extended hours working. I believe tiredness was a contributing factor that led to the death of Stephen - a Tower Bridge probationer police officer. Stephen had worked the extended early turn station shift the previous day and was riding his motorbike to work to start his second extended hours early turn when he misjudged a roadside kerbstone, causing him to crash and suffer serious head injuries from which he did not recover.

The accident had happened not more than 100 yards from Tower Bridge police station, leaving a nasty taste for us all to live with for some time to come. Not nice. An unsung statistic that found no place in published Notting Hill data.

Most marches and demonstrations passed noisily through relatively peacefully. Loud hailers and repeated chants were an everyday occurrence. One particular verse that would be repeatedly sung went like this.

There are no racists in Britain

And coppers never lie.

And Enoch's an Angel

And pigs can fly.

It made me laugh when I heard this as it reminded me of a poem called. 'Babylon Reviewed' written by Harry Awty, one of my tutors at training school. The poem is about how people see the police and contains the word PIGS that stood for 'PRIDE, INTEGRITY & GUTS'.

Pride, integrity, and guts was something all the police officers present had in abundance. So, in a perverse way, the marchers were paying us all a compliment rather than an insult.

I served two Notting Hill Carnival attachments with the 'M' Division – the first was in 1977 and the second in 1978.

In 1977 as part of a 20 strong serial, we paraded early and were immediately sent for operational feeding. Our transport for the day was a green police coach, built to contain stick insects; we all somehow got into it, where we were scrunched up like cattle sitting on rock hard seats with decidedly less than economy seat legroom. Off to be fed at some Territorial Army barracks where if you were lucky enough, the food would be hotter than just warm. Still getting into and out of the coach was the only type of occasional exercise we could take until such time as the proverbial hit the fan, and we would be sent somewhere to test our bottle heading skills as we vied for who controlled the playing field with the locals.

Back on the coach after feeding, we were deployed to 'ground assigned,' which is when the long wait began. If you were lucky, you'd pass the time playing cards, although even playing cards gets monotonous after hours and hours, and you knew that very soon you would be called into action, and like a coiled spring, you would just get up and do it. The reality was that with legs long dead from the lack of movement, we could just about stand up for the first minute or so, and how we never fell over was mainly due to the way we were packed together like sardines. Our time for action was fast approaching, and sure enough, sometime towards the evening, the control room (known as GT) called us forward into the streets of Notting Hill.

We debussed or perhaps more accurately fell out of our confined box like a set of dominoes; we deployed across a road to deny access to would-be rioters. Rioters were usually easy to spot as they normally went around in large groups carrying bricks, bottles and anything else that could be easily launched from a safe distance which they then discharged with some force into the bunched ranks of police officers. This time was no different, and true to form, bricks and bottles began being thrown in our direction. Help was on hand in the form of a shield serial that deployed to our front to protect us from frontal projectiles.

Our protectors had deployed none too soon as a bottle from the rioters came flying over the shield wall, hitting the metal crown on the top of my cork helmet, which then bounced off to hit the poor bugger behind. I took some satisfaction from the fact I had taken the sting out of the bottle, which slowed it sufficiently to prevent it from hitting him with an injury-causing blow. It was while we were being subjected to randomly thrown missiles that a uniformed Superintendent came along and said, "Are you boys going to stand here and take all that. Go forward and sort them out." No need to be told a second time – off we went in pursuit, clearing our tormentors out as we did so – no contest, really. That was until a Chief Superintendent countermanded the orders we had been previously given and sent us back to our original position, where we became the shooting gallery targets for a renewed assault. We held our ground for a few minutes when they blow me down with a feather the Superintendent, who had told us to advance, originally returned to find us in the same position.

"What are you boys doing here? I told you to go and sort them out," and with that, we were ordered forward again, ferreting out the baddies as we did so. There we were enjoying life when the Chief Superintendent returned to send us back to where we had just come from. This happened on no fewer than four occasions, back and forth we went, going up and down the road like a pair of whores draws, and all because no one could make a decision and stick to it.

I think the rioters must have got fed up with us and moved on because our front suddenly became quiet, and we were told to rebus before being redeployed to another location. Whilst en-route, we happened upon two youths busily pulling a woman off a moped looking to steal her handbag, which was held by a strap that crossed her body.

With the word 'stop' being shouted at the driver by everybody on board, the coach stopped immediately, and those at the rear managed to de-bus through the rear door and run to the woman's aid. So, intent on their prey, the youths were not aware of our approach until we were practically in striking distance. I think they would have both got away scot-free, but for the fact, one slipped on the floor sprawling slightly in front of us, a slip that delayed him just long enough for Andy to kick him cleanly in the ribs with a size ten boot. It must certainly have hurt him, though not sufficiently enough to stop him from running off. I'd put money the youth who got kicked didn't much feel like taking any more liberties that night; summary justice, maybe.

Luckily the moped woman was unhurt, and after dusting her down, she was able to get back on her moped and go on her way. No time to take details, our services were required urgently elsewhere to support other under fire officers, and so off we jolly well went. That year the violence pretty much fizzled out for us after that even though we were kept on long into the night. Just in case.

The next year, i.e., 1978, was going to be a bit different. The lessons the police had received the year before were well and truly learnt, and this time around, we were prepared. My serial was collected in a green coach as before, but after operational feeding, we were taken straight to a requisitioned school in the centre of Notting Hill that was to be our operational base for the next two days. Stores were built up, and that included large quantities of food and an old film projector that played 35mm reels of films in the school hall to keep us amused. The film 'Zulu,' where under siege soldiers were being remorselessly attacked, was one of the films being shown that year. There were some similarities between the film and the position we now found ourselves in. Like the defenders at Rorke's Drift, we were both surrounded on all four sides, with a small but still significant proportion of the population looking to 'beat us up. One big difference was that we didn't have any 'Martini-Henry' rifles with bayonets to use to keep them at bay.

The one word that remained in my head from that film was the word '*Usuthu*' shouted by the Zulu warriors as they banged their assegais on their cowhide shields when they ran forward to attack the defenders. There was no doubt that the Zulus were first class, brave warriors, and if it was good enough for them to shout '*Usuthu*,' it must certainly be good enough for the police. With the film now over, we stayed in our 'ground assigned corral' until sure enough, just as it started getting dark, it kicked off again. This time though, we were equipped with shields and wore special helmets fitted with bicycle hardhat type chin straps that kept our helmets on our heads. Bring it on. Our shield serial was deployed against a group of rioters who threw whatever came to hand – bricks, bottles, lumps of wood, bins and so on in our direction. An invitation if ever there was for us to advance in their direction and 'Give them some. And advance is exactly what we did except now as we moved forward, we all used our truncheons to bang on our shields, whilst at the same time we shouted the Zulu war cry of 'Usuthu' as we did so. Cowards that they were the rioters were not too keen on mixing it '*manno et manno*' and ran away. We waited around until the small hours again, and when it was deemed suitable, we went back to our beds for a well-earned sleep. Job done!

---ooo0ooo---

Chapter 27

New Year's Eve in Trafalgar Square

In 1977 and 1978, not only did I get caught for the Notting Hill Carnival, but also for the New Year's Eve celebrations in Trafalgar Square. I hated every minute of the time I spent policing Trafalgar Square – Give me the Battles of Notting Hill any day. I hated it so much that I vowed I would never police Trafalgar Square on New Year's Eve ever again, a promise I managed to keep for the remainder of my service.

Policing New Year's Eve was a completely different barrel of fish to policing at Notting Hill. True, there were no rioters throwing bricks and bottles at us, but give me that any day to just standing there whilst literally hundreds of thousands of drunken revellers celebrated the birth of the 'New Year' with a bang, which I'm sure looking at the state of them plenty of them got.

Being posted to Trafalgar Square felt like you were a parent dealing with petulant children, and it seemed that you were constantly telling them to get off of traffic lights or some other roadside furniture, and if not that, then for them to stop misbehaving or committing some drunken misdemeanour. Most of those, it seemed to me, were women. The number who came past and demanded a 'kiss for the New Year' was ridiculous. Women officers suffered the same fate being kissed by men and women – a double whammy. Now you may think I am some type of Bah humbug but when you are stone-cold sober and everyone else is inebriated to different levels being in uniform in Trafalgar Square is the last place a police officer wants to be. I could empathise with the Victor Meldrew character and his catchphrase, "I don't believe it." In certain circumstances, I enjoy a drink of wine and beer, but despite being offered copious amounts of alcohol, I never found any difficulty in refusing drinks when wearing my uniform. Sadly, something that could not be said for Maxey, a fellow officer.

Maxey succumbed to the temptation of free booze and got absolutely blotto, eventually collapsing in a heap on the Trafalgar Square pavement, causing an obstruction that revellers had to step over, which is where our irate serial inspector found him languishing. Not a pretty sight. Our inspector detailed two officers to take Maxey, a pretty much dead weight, back to the coach - no easy task as it meant dragging him through thousands of revellers. I dread to think what those officers would have done had Maxey chundered over them en route, or for that matter, the remainder of the serial had they returned to a splattered coach. Luckily for Maxey, that never happened, and once in the coach, he was left to sleep it off.

Maxey's reckoning would come a few days later, and I don't think him saying, "Happy New Year" to the Commander would cut too much ice. Probably not the best way for him to start the New Year, but as the French say, "*C'est la vie.*"

---ooo0ooo---

Chapter 28

Probationer Attachments

Police probationer training involved sampling the work of other police units, which meant being sent on attachment. Clearly, some units like the mounted branch, for example, were not included; even if they had been, I would have needed a Shire horse to sit on – something the police were a bit short of. That said, I did complete attachments to the Thames Division based at Wapping, the stations Criminal Investigation Department (CID), and capped it all with a month's posting as a plainclothes observer on the area car.

For my Thames Division attachment, I was sent one sunny day to Thames Wapping in East London. On arrival at the front desk, I was taken through to the workshops, where I hoped to see the up-to-date cutlass training arena, similar to that used by Spartacus and co. Surely, they needed to hone their sword skills to tackle the pirate bands looting and pillaging in wild abandon. Sadly, that had stopped years before; now, they were armed with a piece of wood the same as me. As part of my induction, I was shown around the boatyard and given a potted history of how it all began. Basically, in 1798, the Port of London was being torn apart by waterborne thieves and vagabonds, so the water police were set up to patrol the wharves in whalers to sort out the baddies. That's pretty much how it remained until 1839, when it became part of the Metropolitan Police Force.

Change was not restricted to the police force as over time, the Port of London docks that once heaved with merchant's vessels closed, culling crime and river traffic in the process. There was no comparison to what the police officers back then did. They physically manned oared whalers to get about unlike the modern-day Thames policeman whose sole exertions were to press a button and occasionally turn the boat steering wheel. That said, they banged on about their expertise in recovering decomposing bodies, making out they were some kind of supermen. My view was they were pretty much overpaid mortuary assistants who got extra dough when they took a set of fingerprints from a bloated corpse. As an aside, they also rescued people from drowning and reported marine traffic for such heinous crimes as causing 'a dangerous swirl.' Really can't say it ticked my box, still I was there for the day, so I decided to make the most of it with a free ride up and down the river, copping a tan in the process, and after such a stressful day what could be better than to get back to the station and have a pint in the 'Town of Ramsgate' public house just off Wapping High Street, before catching a train home.

It was during my history lesson that an urgent matter came in which my boat crew were going to deal with post-haste. Now with something to do, we hot-footed (well, slowly walked really) to the jetty and got into a police boat, where I took my seat by the flag at the back. No longer a landlubber, we cast off, and with blue lights flashing, we chugged away towards a Liberian freighter moored in Greenwich. I waited to be told what the urgent matter was we had been sent on – maybe to recover a dead body, or rescue a person from the water, maybe even to arrest someone. I didn't have long to wait as we arrived alongside the registered Liberian freighter where the police pilot sounded a bit like Captain Birds Eye as he shouted out something like 'ahoy their shipmates' after which he climbed a rope ladder and disappeared over the handrails from view. Whilst the boat idled in the water; my mind continued churning over the possibilities – maybe a drug job. The police pilot returned a few minutes later.

My bubble burst when I was eventually told what this urgent matter was. Apparently, the whole boat's crew had gone out for a good few drinks that culminated with them spending a lot of money to enjoy themselves one after the other with the same lady of the night in what could be loosely termed a gang bang. The lady was a willing occupant, who being of a kind and considerate nature, decided that she give each and every one of them a present to remember her by; one that would require a visit to the doctor, followed by a course of penicillin and a two-week abstinence from sex to put right. Now I don't know how this information came into police possession, but it had now been passed on to the freighter captain, who was none too pleased as it meant a delayed sailing to allow his crew to be checked out medically.

So, this was what these 'supermen' did for a living. Our excitement for the day was over; I spent the rest of it sunning myself on the backbench whilst being leisurely chauffeured up and down the Thames. God, it was hell, but someone had to do it. Luckily, not me.

My one week's attachment with Tower Bridge CID was a complete bore. Nothing to get my teeth into; it would have made Thames Division officers look like workaholics. Fortunately, there was one investigation considered so foul and dastardly by the Detective Inspector (DI) that he instigated his own major investigation to find the culprit. This foul and dastardly crime was uncovered when the DI came into the office early one morning and, to his horror, found a bum print clearly visible on his desk's protective glass top. Two pert naked cheek prints were straddling his working space. The shape and size of the bum print led him to believe it belonged to a female, and once that conclusion had been reached, it meant that some unauthorised hanky-panky had occurred during the night, and it was something he had to bottom out.

With the cunning eked from his days at the cutting edge, the DI greeted every CID and crime squad officer as they entered the CID office with the words, "Come with me." That's when he led them into his office, pointing out the offending bum mark and saying in his soft Scottish lilt, "See you, Jimmy. Was that you? Was it eh! You can tell me yeah." The DI wasn't getting very far with his enquiry until a detective called Mick came into the office. When questioned, he freely admitted to how the bum print got there, even offering up the details of who it belonged to. Mick had used the DI's office to have a discreet liaison with a female officer, not realising that he had left evidence to what had gone on. It was lucky for him that it was not a biological trail he had left behind, as that would have incurred a much more serious fine than he was about to get. Thankfully the major enquiry was scaled down, and Mick was taken into the DI's office for a full debriefing on the previous evening's events, something for which the DI fined him a good drink.

Mick had experienced the importance of Locard's basic principle at first hand because 'when two objects meet, there is an exchange from one to another.' The learning he took from this was to be more careful in the future when choosing his hanky-panky sites.

It was during my month's plainclothes observer attachment on the response car that I came across the same

Peter I had met previously in the charge room. Peter was wanted again on a no-bail warrant, and with my fellow crew members, I got out to arrest him. Despite being in plain clothes, I was still required to have my truncheon with me, although, unlike police trousers that have an inbuilt truncheon pocket to sheath, it's 12 inches in I didn't. It might fit in my underpants, but that might be uncomfortable. So, with nowhere else to put it, I held it in my hand. Now Peter and his elder brother Michael were extremely close and known to be of a violent disposition. In fact, both had been involved in a violent attack on an Isle of Wight police officer for which Michael served a three-year prison sentence.

Peter was now under arrest and was seated in the back of a police van, and yours truly was standing outside the van, still holding my truncheon, when Peter's elder brother Michael arrived, carrying in his right hand a lager bottle by its neck. Once Michael saw Peter in the van, he came walking towards us, carrying the bottle in an aggressive manner. That's when he looked at me, and my mind instantly went into 'Oh sugar mode' or something like that, increasing in thoughts as he called out to Peter, "Peter, have you been hit by the guy with the club.' There was a heart-stopping moment until, thankfully, Peter said, "No, I'm not hurt." That's when Michael dropped the bottle on the ground and was promptly arrested for possessing an offensive weapon joining his brother in the back of the police van.

Phew, that was a close call. Had Peter given a different answer, I think I would have been the recipient of some rather serious unwanted attention from a man armed with a bottle. I made damned certain thereafter that my truncheon was kept close at hand but discreetly concealed up my sleeve well out of sight until needed. As they say, 'out of sight, out of mind;' it might just give me the edge some time.

---ooo0ooo---

Chapter 29

Provost

One night duty saw Hips driving an unmarked crime car with Vulch riding shotgun. Sometime during the night, Hips picked up a car that was being driven erratically along the Old Kent Road from the Elephant and Castle area towards Blackheath. Hips got behind the vehicle and, using the car's bell and flashing his lights; he requested it to stop. The driver of the car refused to do so, and next thing you know, he had accelerated away in an effort to lose them, and a chase ensued along the Old Kent Road that continued through New Cross and Deptford, along towards the traffic lights at the foot of Blackheath Hill. That's where it all went pear-shaped. The bandit car decided to ram into the police car that had by now come alongside them at the junctions red traffic lights. This ramming locked both vehicles together, effectively closing the road in all directions. Both the driver and the passenger were arrested on suspicion of taking a motor vehicle without consent and as the driver had been drinking he was also arrested for driving a vehicle whilst under the influence of alcohol.

An accident of this type is known as a 'POLACC' (Police Accident), which means it has to be reported at the scene by a traffic division garage sergeant. It meant that Hips remained at the scene to report the accident whilst a station van attended and collected Vulch and the two prisoners and conveyed them back to the charge room at Tower Bridge, where they were sheeted. That is where they were joined a while later by Hips and the garage sergeant to complete the accident report in full.

Enquiries revealed the two prisoners were serving British soldiers. This meant that once our police enquiries were completed, they would be released into the custody of the Provost Marshalls Office – not something that was going to be to their advantage. The driver was dealt with under the breathalyser procedure, with a doctor being called and a blood sample taken. The blood analysis would be known at a later date, so on that matter, the driver was bailed to another date.

Enquiries were still ongoing regarding the car, so they were both placed in the cell until these were completed. Luckily for them, the vehicle came back, not stolen. They were not out of the woods yet, because now we notified the Provost Marshalls Office, who turned up 30 minutes or so later in an army vehicle which they parked in the station yard. The provost that turned up that day were three of the biggest bruisers I have ever seen. They were that big; they had to duck and turn sideways as they came through the charge room door.

The Provost Sergeant had a quiet chat with the station officer to find out what the circumstances of the arrest were. He was none too impressed when he was told the driver had deliberately rammed a police car. "Oh, he did, did he?" Once the formalities had been completed, the errant soldiers were brought out of the cells and handed into the custody of the provost marshals. It was only when they were stuck in handcuffs that I noticed their ashen faces and the fact that they were quite literally quaking in their boots. I didn't blame them for that, especially after they had been told by the top honcho present that 'pretty soon they would be very, very, very sorry.' The threat being conveyed in those few words spoke volumes – they would both soon be getting a good beating. And it wasn't long in coming, as they were each cuffed across the head and made to apologise in person to Hips and Vulch for the inconvenience they had caused.

Then to the sounds of 'Stand to attention' followed by 'quick march,' the two errant soldiers were frog marched to the army vehicle and taken away to whatever fate awaited them in the Provost Marshalls cells. I genuinely felt sorry for those two as I knew they were about to be given a good 'licking.' Perhaps next time, they will stop and think before acting so irresponsibly.

---ooo0ooo---

Chapter 30

Why is a Policeman's lot so little?

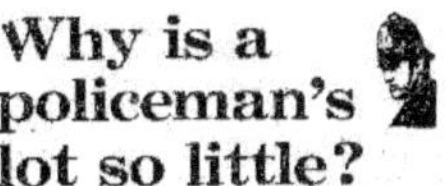

During my probation, police pay and conditions were two hot topic news items. Contrary to popular belief, police pay and conditions at that time were not particularly good. They were so bad that rumours were circulating amongst the rank-and-file members about the possibility of a 'Police Strike' taking place. Police strikes had occurred in 1918 and 1919, so it was not something unheard of, except that following the last police strike, the Government of the day took steps to prevent strikes from occurring in the future. The steps taken involved the creation of the Police Federation, an independent organisation not affiliated to any political party or the trade union movement that would act as a vehicle to address policing issues. On its creation, rank and file police officers lost the right to strike.

Clearly then, if the police decided to call a 'strike,' it would have been against the law. That said, had all the police phoned in sick at the same time, that would not have been against the law and would have had pretty much the same effect. The talk was about a unified day of sickness, so things were beginning to get a bit heated.

And so, it was sometime towards the end of 1977 I decided to write a letter to add my voice to the growing debate about police pay, conditions and the possibility of a police strike. Putting pen to paper, I wrote a letter with my name and contact details on to a National Newspaper which they printed under the title 'Why is a policeman's lot so little?'

The letter read:

'I am a police officer with a year's service in the Metropolitan Police, allegedly the highest paid force in the country. I have just opened my monthly pay advice, and for a full month's duty, I netted £148.78." For this, I have worked seven night duties (inclusive of weekends). I finished night duty at 6:00 a.m. on Monday and was required to resume work at 1:45 p.m. that same day. I am allowed one weekend and six days off a month. Apart from night duty, I work seven late turn shifts (02:00 p.m. – 10:00 p.m.) and seven early turn shifts (6:00 a.m. – 2:00 p.m.). For working bank holidays, I get double time and no day off in lieu. All my duties are subject to change (including weekly leaves). Three months ago, I was seriously injured and had to go to the hospital. My case is in no way unique. A single colleague

of mine with eight years of service received a net wage of £198. I am, to put it mildly, disillusioned to hear that the government does not consider us a special case'. David Glenister London W

I'd like to think that maybe my letter was the catalyst that forced the Government's hand to look more closely into this issue. Either way, it's now a matter of fact that in 1978 the then Labour Government commissioned a review into police pay and conditions led by Lord Edmund-Davies. The recommendations he made in that review were implemented in 1979 when the Thatcher Government came to power – a good time for me as I got something like a 40% pay rise overnight.

With pay increases still a distant possibility, I still had to pay the bills on the money I was earning on a monthly basis and to do that, I needed to work whatever overtime became available; unfortunately, that meant sacrificing my precious monthly weekend off. Even that was difficult to arrange because you had to beat the old sweat nine to fivers who were the first ones informed when weekend working requirements became known. The only ones they never volunteered for were the ones they thought might turn violent, as that meant they might get hurt.

I was lucky then to be in the admin office when volunteers were required to police the 1979 Nottingham Forest versus Southampton League Cup Final at Wembley stadium. Straight away, I put Ghurkha and myself on the aid sheet, which is how we became part of an 'M' Division serial, pretty much the young guys on the block with the rest made up of old sweat police officers. They had only volunteered so they could get into Wembley Stadium for free, watch the game and be paid for the privilege in the process. Nice way to spend your day. I suspect, as far as they were concerned, "work' was an ugly word. They had plans, so they wanted to start at 9:00 a.m. and finish at 6 p.m. so they could get home in time for tea. Making arrests were definitely a no-no.

Parading in the Southwark canteen, we got onto our coach and went straight away to operational feeding, after which we were deployed to our assigned area. Boy, were the old sweats upset when our serial was posted to exterior crowd control. This meant they would not be able to get inside the stadium to watch the game, despite them trying all means they could to somehow get into the stadium – urgent toilet needs and such like – all excuses fell on deaf ears. I suppose, for sheer persistence, they all at the very least deserved an 'A' for effort.

The match was closely fought, swinging one way and then the other before Nottingham Forest came out on top, winning the match 3 – 2. It would have been a good game to watch something the old sweats moaned about as we pretty much sat the whole game on our coach. That was until we were sent to deal with a crowd disturbance on Wembley Way – something definitely not in the old sweats grand scheme of things – not by a country mile. Ghurkha and I, by contrast, were in our element, thankful to be able to get our teeth into real police work. Once deployed on scene, our serial debussed into a regular melee of small fights breaking out among the rival fans. Not surprisingly, whilst the old sweats conveniently turned a blind eye, Ghurkha and I got stuck in and arrested a Nottingham Forest fan for assault and public order offences. One in the bin, we waited what seemed like hours for a van to arrive and take us to a nearby police station to process our prisoner, one of a fair number who had been arrested. The sheer number descending at once meant the time taken to process our prisoner took a lot longer than it normally would take.

That delay meant the rest of our serials had to patiently wait for us both to re-join them before they could be dismissed and sent home. Ghurkha and I were inwardly pleased with our performance, although the same can't be said for the old sweats because when we re-joined the coach, we found them pretty much seething. They made their views known verbally as we sat down to calls of W-----s and a few other names to boot. They were now extremely late for the meals they had pre-booked (their fault, not ours), which by now were either dried up, been fed to the dog or had simply been binned. As an aside, after the episode, the old sweats

never volunteered for work on a serial that we were part of
- their loss – our gain.

Learning curve – when doing the right thing, the baddies
are not the only ones who get upset – C'est la vie.

---ooo0ooo---

Chapter 31

Christmas at the Drum

It was an annual event at the 'Drum' that the residents were treated to a free Christmas dinner and drink served in the canteen in the early evening. The wine was served by the bottle, and beer was available from the keg. Certainly not an event to miss unless, of course, you happened to be working the 2 p.m. – 10 p.m. late turn shift. Now whether I was just being plain unlucky, it seemed I was dipping out on this 'freebie' because, for two years running, the meal had been held when I was otherwise engaged on duty at Tower Bridge.

The last missed meal was in 1978 when after a busy late turn, JT and I arrived in the Drum canteen for something to eat to find Phyllis, the duty canteen lady, three parts to the wind, a bit tipsy, to say the least. The dirty tables left behind by the fortunate ones were a testament to the fact that the Christmas dinner was long finished. Phyllis could talk, although he was not really in any position to stand up. As all the food and drink that night was free, we were invited to help ourselves to whatever goodies had been left behind in the food and beer stakes. Never one to miss an opportunity like this we searched high and low and found to our surprise two unopened bottles of wine in the fridge which the canteen staff had sorted away for themselves to drink later.

When we returned from the kitchen area back to the canteen, we had the two bottles of now open wine that never touched the sides as we drank them down in short order before going to our pits for a good night's sleep. It was not until the next day that we were notified of a theft allegation of two bottles of wine that had been made by the canteen manageress to Greenwich Police. The matter was going to be personally investigated by the 'R' Division Commander. It followed then that, along with JT and a fellow PC named Lew (not sure why he was named), we were unceremoniously summoned from our relief duties and ordered to appear before the Commander post haste at his office. Doing as requested, we presented ourselves at his offices where like naughty schoolboys, we appeared before him as a group. Clearly, this allegation was being taken seriously because he had a Superintendent lap dog with him as a witness should charges or discipline proceedings ensue.

Commander 'R' started with, "I am told you stole two bottles of wine from the section house canteen. You entered an area you were not supposed to as trespassers, which makes this a burglary. If that is correct, you are all an absolute disgrace. What have you got to say about this allegation." It seemed to me that he looked squarely at me for an answer, so I answered him. "Well, sir, we did take the wine, but this officer here," pointing at Lew, "was not a party to it."

Commander 'R' now looking at Lew 'Is that right.' Lew nodded his head in agreement, and with no words such as 'Sorry' being used, he was dismissed and sent from the room.

Now it was just the four of us in the room. Commander R told me to continue, so I said 'Well sir, firstly we were invited to enter the canteen kitchen area by the canteen assistant, so we did not enter as trespassers, and secondly, the bottles of wine were ours to drink in the first place which means we have committed no crime whatsoever. It appears the only offence here has been committed by the canteen staff who stole our wine in the first place'. My face clearly showed I was pleased with my response as the Commander responded. "Don't get clever with me, and take that smirk off your face.'

That's when Commander R, a very down to earth person, used some pretty salty language. Venting his spleen to empty, he gave us both a severe dressing down about our outrageous behaviour, which he interspersed liberally with the threat of possible discipline and dismissal. This was serious stuff for me, as I was still a month or so shy of being confirmed in the office of a police constable. I knew I was in a vulnerable position, and this threat was not something I took lightly. So, I waited patiently for the tirade to finish, fighting the urge to stand my ground, and when a suitable opportunity arose, I apologised profusely for my lack of judgment. That's when the Commander dismissed me from the room. JT as a senior police officer was kept about 10 minutes longer, during which his fortunes were read out to him in graphic detail. Pretty much lots of hot air and blustering from the Commander over something that was not even a crime.

It's a pity the Commander never investigated the theft of police shirts from the section house drying room with such vigour. No, such mundane matters were left with the local CID to deal with. These allegations were made so frequently that on the last occasion, the local CID contacted every 'Drum' resident requesting a duty statement from them. This was a nonsense request, so I responded likewise with a signed and dated statement that simply read 'I wasn't here.'

Before I leave this section, there was one issue that made me very angry at the double standards senior police officers used to deal with police complaints. I had already experienced first-hand the way senior officers were only too ready to take the word of a complainant at face value, where the investigation as far as they were concerned was a done deal. Forget the evidence we were all guilty in their eyes - Not a particularly good way to approach an investigation, but then maybe those senior officers were FLUBA's short for Flipping Lazy Useless B-----s, who didn't have the investigating skills to do a thorough job. It seemed that they had forgotten the basic rules of evidence because police officers subject to internal discipline have the same entitlements to be treated no differently to members of the public.

That sadly was something manifestly missing when the police received a complaint made by a mayor's office on behalf of the mayor's chauffeur against two unknown police officers. The claim was that these two officers had abused their authority and, for good measure, had insulted the mayor's driver in the process. The chauffeur had apparently been stopped in Southwark by a blue police V8 Rover wireless car that contained a sergeant and a constable. The mayor's driver had been forcefully told in no uncertain terms to move the official car from where it was parked as it was causing an obstruction. The threat of arrest reinforced this request, and as you can imagine, with discretion being the better part of valour, the driver acquiesced and moved off to another location. The fact the car was causing an obstruction was conveniently glossed over. Either way, it meant the mayor's official car was not there to collect him from the function, something the mayor took exception to, so using his mayoral powers, he lodged an official complaint. I can just imagine what was said when the complaint was received by some high-ranking sycophant; probably something like yes, Mr Mayor; no, Mr Mayor;

three bags full, Mr Mayor; absolutely outrageous behaviour, Mr Mayor, etc. as he slowly bowed out of his mayoral presence to trace the culprits.

The investigation started and stopped when a check on the Southwark station duties showed an 'M Division' blue rover wireless car had been crewed that particular night by a sergeant and a constable. It must be them – case solved. Unfortunately for the investigating officer, both officers, when interviewed under caution, didn't play ball and denied any knowledge of the incident. Suitably put out, the investigating officer took exception, asking himself the questions 'Surely this cannot be, how dare they deny this heinous crime?' With that, he pulled his masterstroke and asked both officers whether they would stand on an ID parade – something they readily agreed to, and two identification parades were arranged where the two suspects paraded in uniform alongside their uniform colleagues. The investigating officer then briefed the witness up with the usual walk up and down the parade pitch and left him to it. Guess what? The chauffeur couldn't pick anyone out.

Now in cases like this, it's normal to discharge the parade, and that's it. The investigating officer had his chance and blew it. Unfortunately, he was still in a fit of pique and not thinking straight, so he disregarded identification procedure rules and went with the witness up to the two suspected officers, in turn, touching them on the arm, saying, "could this be the person?' Even then, the witness could not identify them. This incident left a sour taste in my mouth. It just showed that the investigating officer had decided the mayor's driver was telling the truth, and that was that – it was a case of there's no smoke without fire – forget about the honesty and integrity part. The end result of all these investigations, apart from a lot of paperwork and the waste of police time and cost, was – absolutely nothing happened.

Learning curve: refer to Rule 1 - Trust no one, especially senior officers, and Rule 2 - never let your guard down – simple things can develop into serious issues if you are not careful.

---ooo0ooo---

Chapter 32

Southall Riots

It's funny, but you did not have to volunteer for some aid postings; you were just assigned. The National Front meeting being held in Southall was a point in question as the 'MT' contingent seemed to have been cherry-picked from the station relief rosters. It was funny that the old sweats were the only ones missing, an early indication if ever there was that this was perhaps going to get a bit perky. We paraded at Southwark Police Station where our serial of an inspector, two sergeants, and twenty constables was joined by similar-sized serial who we would be working alongside. It was when we were briefed that we found out our serials were designated as non-shield. This effectively meant we would be the first officers deployed to police the demonstrators. We would therefore become the first to experience incoming missiles when it all went bent, a sort of "cannon fodder" early warning system when the proverbial hit the fan. After the briefing, we went out to our transport - a large 50 seat 'grey-green' rented coach. Compared to the small green 23-seat coaches, this one was the height of luxury with nice comfortable seats, plenty of legroom, and large windows that provided ample light and vision.

We were like condemned men as we went to eat our last hot meal. Clearly, it was going to be a long day as we also collected additional refreshments, such as drinks and sandwiches, and a large portable radio for receiving and sending messages to GT or Broadway. That's when we were sent to our operational park-up area, a road perhaps 400 yards from the hall where the National Front Meeting was to be held. Some of our colleagues were already deployed as a uniform cordon in front of the hall. We played cards as we sat and waited, during which time the number of Anti-National Front protesters started to arrive and stand in front of the police cordon protecting the hall. Now we could see that this cordon stretched from a flat-roofed four-story building across the road to another building. Police horses and a number of shield serials were held in reserve behind this cordon.

From the top of the flat-roofed building silhouetted against the skyline were a gaggle of senior police officers, safely out of harm's way and now blessed with a panoramic overview of the scene immediately below them. One of them was in possession of a loud hailer.

The stream of Anti-National Front demonstrators standing in front of the police cordon had steadily grown to somewhere in the region of about 500 or so in a group about five deep. That's when one of the bright sparks on the roof had a Eureka moment. He decided that if we deployed the two 'M' Division serials behind these 500 demonstrators, they would be the filling in the sandwich, effectively penned in and therefore would not be able to cause trouble. The orders to deploy us were sent, and so with our colleagues holding the front cordon, we traipsed off our coach and created the rear cordon as planned. It was a masterstroke - well, at least until over 1000 more protesters arrived, whereby we now had a four-layer sandwich, the filling of which was made up of two ingredients that were not particularly complementary to each other: them and us. It was obvious to us where our salvation lay, and strangely, without orders to do so, we walked through the initial crowd of 500 and joined our colleagues holding the front cordon. The status quo had returned to the same as before we had been deployed, except the police cordon was a little bit thicker than it had been whilst that of the demonstrators had at least trebled in size and was growing exponentially with every passing minute.

It's funny, but when you are placed in situations of stress, you can sense the tension palpably increasing, and yet you can't put your finger on how you know that. That's how it was for the rank-and-file police at Southall; we knew it was going to kick-off, just didn't know when. Sure enough, it started with a few bottles being thrown from deep within the crowd. That was when the loud hailer came into action, where the senior officer on the roof used it, speaking like a first world war pilot with a plum in his mouth saying, "I say chaps, I can see the baddie who threw that bottle. There he is, ten rows in front of you," following up with, "If you rush out now, you'll get him." A few ribald comments were made as to the action we would take, most of it centred on where to stick his loudhailer. What the dingbat on the roof did not consider was that the furthest we could see was two or three rows in front.

Had we decided to 'rush out and get him,' the cordon would have disintegrated completely. I thought back to my days at Hendon and wondered if the person on the roof was the same dingbat who provided such concise instructions on how to stop a horse and, of course, what to do in the event of nuclear war. Loudspeaker man continued to exercise his lungs as we maintained our cordon. During this, a much more serious problem presented itself as our coach had suddenly kicked into life and pulled away from the road where we had left it, starting to accelerate straight towards the demonstrators and of course us. In terms of making the demonstrators move, let me say it worked a treat as they jumped out of the way pretty damn quick or otherwise face being run over. They all chose to get out the way. This action posed a number of questions.

First, 'why was the driver doing this?'

Second, 'how do you stop a runaway coach?'

This was clearly a flaw in police training. After all was said and done, I had been provided with a form 29 and trained to run in the same direction to deal with a runaway horse. However, this was a runaway coach some 40 or so feet long and was now heading straight for me. Reverting back to common sense and my own personal survival mode, the solution came to me in a flash. What's good for the demonstrators is good for me - get out of its way - which was exactly what all my colleagues and I did.

The reason for this somewhat drastic cause of action soon became apparent as the coach drove past us. We could see that the large rear window was now a gaping hole through which a stream of smoke was now exiting through where the window had been. It appeared that some kind person from the anti-national front contingent had decided to torch our coach and cook our civilian coach driver in the process.

That's when things got interesting as the thrown incoming projectiles started to escalate. As we had rightly guessed, we were now in the front line as cannon fodder and would pretty soon start taking casualties. Thankfully, a few shield-trained serials deployed and took over our cordon as we pulled back out of projectile range, with behind us some rather large police horses chomping at the bit to get into action.

As a person who was there in the thick of it, the violence that day directed against the police was more intense than previous demonstrations I had been on. It placed the rank-and-file officers in an exposed and precarious position where the potential for being seriously hurt was all too evident. Our bacon was saved by the Blue Cobra boys from the Special Patrol Group (SPG) who came from behind us in their vehicles and drove slowly along the road directly at the demonstrators in line abreast using the vehicles driver and passenger doors fully extended like wings, to shield its complement of officers following in close support. The demonstrators were being pushed back, dispersing into small pockets as they did so. The SPG took a lot of bad press that day, effectively being put up as the prime suspects who delivered the blow from which a demonstrator by the name of Blair Peach sadly died. Personally, as a person who was present at the coal face so to speak, I firmly believe that their intervention on that day saved a lot of people, me in particular from suffering serious harm.

So, albeit a bit belated, I unreservedly thank them all for their help that day.

---ooo0ooo---

Chapter 33

Car Pound

The police car pound at Pages Walk was used to store cars that had been removed for some reason or other, usually for breaching parking regulations. The car pound was operated on a 24-hour basis and, as such, had a full-time police compliment made up of a sergeant, four police officers, and a number of traffic wardens. The sergeant managed the day to day running of the car pound, although as the car pound was on Tower Bridges manner technically, its control was managed by the Tower Bridge duty officer, who visited the car pound during each shift to check the money collected tallied up with the number of vehicles returned to their owner. Apart from the daily attendance of the duty officer, the car pound was pretty much a self-supporting unit that needed little or no support from relief officers except when the cover was needed for sickness or annual leave.

That was where the real problem lay because none of us had received any official training as to what we had to do when posted to work at the car pound. The basic training should at the very least have been on how to use the cash register, but no; it was just accepted that you would be able to do it – no small feat since we didn't know what 'it' entailed.

I turned up for work for duty this one night to find I had been given this task as the usual officer had gone sick. There was no 'Mission Impossible' taped introduction like 'This mission should you choose to accept it' it was more a case of Hobson's choice when Torchy the duty officer said 'Daisy, you're up the car pound tonight. Get yourself up there and relieve the late turn officer. There is a traffic warden working there, so I don't expect any problems. I'll be up to see you about 05:00 a.m. so you can make me a cup of tea then.' Not much I could say to that except 'Okay' and off I went to the car pound. There, I relieved the late turn PC, after which I asked the traffic warden what I had to do.

At the words of 'Just leave everything to me, love' I checked out the car pound porta cabin. It was nothing grand although there were toilets, the sergeant's office, a kitchen area/restroom (complete with television), and of course, the reception office and public waiting area. The reception itself was built like a bank teller's station, with a glass barrier frontage between you and the person you were serving. On our side (obviously) were a credit card swipe machine and a cash register that contained a float of money and the day's takings of cash and credit card receipts. The whole operation was about taking payment, completing the relevant car documents and updating the vehicle's location status on the police national computer. That was it, and since the traffic wardens sorted this out, I didn't need to get too excited about doing anything except to deal with any troublesome customers. Job done; I made myself comfortable in the kitchen area and turned on the television to feast my eyes on a program or two or three, and maybe if I was lucky to catch a few hours' kip.

My plans didn't quite go as I planned because one thing Torchy nor, for that matter, the traffic warden had told me was her hours of duty. Am I a mind reader? Unless I'm told how was I to know she only worked until midnight and what's more to the point I only found that out when the traffic warden bang on midnight came into the kitchen and said to me 'I'm going now, bye' and off she jolly well went. So exactly at 1 minute past midnight, I was on my lonesome where I would remain until being relieved at 06:00 a.m. Now six hours may not seem a long time, but when someone could arrive at any minute, and you didn't have a Scooby what to do - it can seem like a lifetime.

Sod's law was that when the car owners came out of the theatre or some other place and found their cars missing, the first port of call would be to call the police and either report the car as stolen or be told where the vehicle had been removed from and taken to. That's when they would hail a cab and come straight over. Sure enough, I wasn't to be disappointed as between 12 midnight and three in the morning; I was as busy as hell dealing with one irate car owner after another as they turned up to reclaim their precious car. I could only restore a car if a person could

a) prove who they were

b) they had ownership of the car and

c) whether they were able to pay in full the removal fee and storage cost.

There was a payment grace period allowed for those who were not able to pay at the time. That was pretty much a judgment call, made at the time by the car pound staff. Some had no I.D. or documentation to prove who they were, so they were easy to deal with. They were sent away with a flea in their ear to obtain the documentation required.

Those that had documentation usually made a few moans and groans whilst completing their paperwork, although still coughed up the money, which I sort of banked in the cash till. After that, they were shown out to their vehicle, which once the barrier was raised, they drove off into the night. Everything was hunky-dory until Torchy turned up and started to work out how many cars had been restored against the payment I had taken. That was when it all fell apart. They never matched up. What should have been a simple, oh-so-simple task turned into a marathon. It looked like I had either over or undercharged the car owners. My data entries were all incorrect, with even something simple like £4.80p suddenly becoming either £4800.00 or £0.48p. Thankfully all the money was accounted for. There was one good thing that came out of it all, and that was that I was never again asked to do car pound relief duties.

It was shortly after this I applied for and was accepted for a posting to the Diplomatic Protection Group (DPG). The decision to apply for the DPG was purely financial as the package on offer was just too good to turn down. Effectively I would get 2 hours a day travelling paid at time and a third, for a guaranteed six months. This totaled the equivalent of 335 hours of pay for doing nothing. As a recently married man, that additional money was a welcome addition to the family coffers being used to offset the bills that were now becoming due. On top of that was the prospect of working overtime which would more than double my monthly take-home pay.

---ooo0ooo---

Chapter 34

Diplomatic Protection Group Posting

1979 - 1980

Rhodesian Conference

Southern Rhodesia (now Zimbabwe) came into being in 1895 during a period of British expansionism propagated by the British politician Cecil Rhodes. Rhodesia was governed by the United Kingdom until it became a self-governing sovereign state following a Unilateral Declaration of Independence in 1965 when Ian Smith became its first and only prime minister. It was the catalyst that started a little shindig that simmered on and off for the next 14 years. During that time, Rhodesia became an international pariah, shunned by all on the international stage where sanctions were imposed on them at a time when they were fighting a guerrilla war against insurgents on two fronts. The first front was a non-violent protest group led by Bishop Abel Muzorewa, and the second was a violent guerrilla movement known as the Patriotic Front, a combined force from the ZANU party led by Robert Mugabe and ZAPU led by

Joshua Nkomo. It was a war of attrition that could only be resolved when all parties agreed to sit down and reach a political solution to the problem. That meeting in September 1979 was to be held at Lancaster House in London chaired by Lord Carrington, the foreign secretary.

How was I to know that this little shindig starting over 7000 miles away when I was 11 years old would soon be heading to London some 14 years later to sort out? It was this single event that meant the DPG needed to expand and expand fast. So, a posting to the DPG was advertised in Police Orders for extra staff.

The DPG remit was to provide an armed response within Central London and to guard cabinet ministers, previous prime ministers, diplomatic premises, and personnel. The potential was there to make a lot of money in a relatively short space of time, although with the Rhodesian Conference coming to town, the potential riches were sure to increase, and I wanted to be part of it.

I completed my application, passed the initial paper shift, and was asked to attend for interview. My only interview experience had been when I attended Paddington on my initial application back in 1976. With the day's events still fresh in my memory, I took every precaution to make sure I wouldn't be caught out with a snap medical or two, so just to be sure, on the day of the interview, I got up really early, had a good hot bath, cleaned my 'never regions,' jumped into a clean pair of shreddies and dressed in a freshly pressed uniform. I needn't have bothered. The interview was a breeze, and in September 1979, I was posted to Walton Street DPG Station (call sign 'Ranger Bravo').

Walton Street was positioned just off Knightsbridge, where we provided armed cover for British politicians that included the then prime minister, Margaret Thatcher; foreign secretary, Lord Carrington, home secretary, William Whitelaw, and Humphrey Atkins, the Northern Ireland secretary as well as that of former prime minister Edward Heath. Apart from our homegrown politicians, we also covered various embassies and consulates, one of which was the Iranian Consulate in Prince's Gate.

The DPG at that time was made up of an eclectic band of police officers on temporary attachment from police divisions around the Metropolitan Police Force area, retaining their divisional numbers as identification. I remained PC293 'M' until I was permanently posted, which is when I would become PC357 DP.

I was not disappointed that when the Rhodesia Conference came to London, it widened the monetary tributary into a veritable stream that ran like a torrent through the Chancellor of the Exchequers Rhodesia Conference Fund. Our pay masters were dishing out money, mainly in overtime, like it was going out of fashion. The Zimbabwe Conference appeared to have brought with it some of the King Solomon's Mines' gold, and a branch had opened up and had now come home to roost right on our doorstep. Not one to look a gift horse in the mouth my colleagues and I took whatever was being offered for as long as we damned well could.

The money tributary started paying out on my first day when all my rest days were cancelled without notice. This meant I would get paid at double time for working my rest days and also get another rest day back in the process. The demand requirements meant officers could not be released to take their re-rostered rest days, so that day too was they would work- this time with notice for which you got paid overtime at time and a half. In short a rest day cancelled without notice was worth three and a half times your daily wage. So just to work two days over a weekend was worth the equivalent of seven days' pay. It was a license to print money, and I obliged them in earning a lot, after all said and done –, a bird in the hand is worth two in the bush. Not knowing when the money stream would dry up, I worked every day for over two months. Each day was a minimum of 10 hours, invariably more. Lovely jubbly, thank you very much.

I use the term 'work' loosely as it mainly involved either sitting down in a comfortable chair or patrolling up and down the pavement for two or so hours, counting paving slabs or cars. It was not the most stimulating job around, but money is a funny thing; it makes it seem all worthwhile.

One of the officers on my relief at Walton Street was one Trevor Lock. Trevor was an advanced police driver with 15 years of experience who was on attachment to the DPG from the K Division. As an advanced driver, Trevor not only took his turn at driving the DPG armed response car Ranger 3 but also covered fixed posts when required. As police do when they meet up, we would exchange stories of past experiences. Trevor had more stories to tell than me, but one story he told me concerned a building site death. Trevor had been called to a building site to deal with a headless torso. There was not much left of the head as it had vanished when the victim had, for some reason, opened the pile driver inspection hatch and stuck his head inside to see whether the pile driver was working. Guess what? It was. Even then, with a head missing from its shoulders, a doctor had to be called to pronounce life extinct.

Traveling to and from Walton Street was no big hassle. I would normally either drive or cycle to Walton Street to parade for work, but on some occasions, I would travel there by train and tube. It was when I decided to travel to work by tube that I came across some ignorant people whose actions made me very angry. I had got onto a tube train and sat down alone on a two-person seat that faced towards an empty two-person seat, minding my own business. At the next stop, two men got into my carriage and sat opposite me. They were not the brightest sparks around because they never recognised, I was a police officer despite being dressed in half blues. One of these two had an open sandwich with him that he took a bite from.

Clearly, it was not to his palate as he said something like 'Yuck', and seconds later, without any warning, he decided to throw the remaining sandwich onto the empty seat alongside me. That was not a good thing to do because that had now made me angry. I decided the most effective way to pass on my displeasure was by taking a practical course of action rather than a lecture, and that's when I stood up from my seat, and in one movement, I picked the sandwich up off the seat, leant over towards chummy and stuffed the sandwich into the man's left-hand jacket pocket, patting it down for good measure as hard as I could so that some of the fillings would stick to the inside lining saying 'Don't do that; it's not nice' as I did so. I think the man was shell shocked as he blurted out the words "Sorry, mate." Needless to say, both he and his friend got off the carriage at the next stop, suitably chastised and taking his sandwich with him. Job done, I remained on the tube until my stop, where I got off and walked to Walton Street.

As a non-firearm trained officer, I was not allowed to man armed posts until I had completed a firearms course, which took a month or so to arrange. It was on my firearms training course that I learned guns were not my forte. Sure, I could hit wooden target sufficient times to pass the course, but my shot groupings were all over the place. I think some of the instructors slept with their guns; they were that good at placing shots. A word of advice is that unless you are trained to an exceptionally high standard, don't challenge a Level 1 trained firearms instructor to a duel; you'll lose.

Sadly, all good things must come to an end, and with my six-month attachment nearing an end, I had to make a decision as to whether to go back to relief duty at Tower Bridge or become a permanent member of the DPG. The money had slowed a bit but was still going strong, so I opted to stay and become PC 357DP.

Walton Street officers were responsible for guarding the Iranian consulate in Princes Gate that was known by its designated call sign as 'Ranger Bravo 14 post.' The consulate was a large terrace building that fronted out onto Hyde Park and the Serpentine. A service road with two entrances gave direct vehicular access and egress onto Kensington Road, Knightsbridge itself. Between the two entrances ran a six-foot-or-so wall that separated the service road from the Knightsbridge pavement area. Its position exposed it to the cold wind that whipped along Knightsbridge, where it mixed with the opposing wind forces coming from the direction of Hyde Park, causing the temperate to plummet to extremes of cold sufficient to freeze the balls off a brass monkey. Even wearing winter woollies did not prevent the wind from cutting through you straight to the bone, and it didn't do much for my matrimonial prospects, which seemed to shrink and disappear from sight.

In these conditions, the hands got so cold that drawing a gun in anger was not really an option. It was no wonder then that this post was affectionately known as 'Ice Station Zebra'. There was not a lot we could do about getting cold save to petition the powers to be to build a centrally heated sentry box, and that was a non-starter, so we were surprised when the Iranian Charge d'affaires provided a typist chair for police officers to sit on within a covered porch between the outer and inner front doors. It was the height of luxury as you were now out of the biting wind. Not a lot happened at any of the DPG fixed posts for the next few months or so. Inactivity can lead to complacency setting in, where you begin to think, '*it wouldn't ever happen to me.*' We were in for a big surprise.

There was nothing particularly special for me about being at work on 30th April 1980 other than my first posting was a long three hour one guarding the Northern Ireland Secretary's home. Once that finished, I was to return to base for a one-hour refreshment break before going out to relieve Trevor at Ranger Bravo 14 post. What I didn't know was that my posting would last a lot, lot, lot longer than the three hours I was scheduled.

This was due to six heavily armed terrorists who for the next six days, became the focus of world media avidly following the unfolding events that became known as the Iranian Embassy Siege. Ironically the fact Trevor was sitting in the porch area probably saved his life. As it was, Trevor opened the external door to the terrorists, who immediately overpowered him and took control of the consulate. The rest, so they say, is history. It ended when the Special Air Service (SAS) forcibly evicted them six days later, on 5th May, leaving five dead in the process. Trevor was later awarded the George Medal for his actions during the siege. For certain, lady luck was on my side on 30th April - there but for the grace of God.

In June, I went on a three-week solo motorcycle course running out of Hendon. To cut a long story short, I did not pass the final ride - yep, a failure! To impart the news officially, I was sent to see the Chief Instructor. The Chief Instructor was an old school Superintendent who had been at the driving school for years. I went into his office to find him sat behind a desk. He was not one to break bad news gently; he just said it as it was. Looking up from his desk, he said, "PC Glenister, It's like this, son. Some of us are good at riding a bike, and some of us are good in bed. I'm good at riding a bike; let's hope your good in bed," and with that, I was dismissed and sent on my way.

On my return to the station, I was posted for a month as a member of the Ranger 500 crew. Ranger 500 was a maroon red transit van that provided the central London armed response capability. As armed officers, we were not supposed to respond to any call other than one involving weapons. It was during this tour that the Ranger 500 crew arrested eight people – no meagre feat and a record that may be still stands to this day.

One arrest for driving unfit was a bit difficult to avoid, really, as we were travelling towards a car that came slowly along Belgrave Road on our side of the road. Thankfully the driver, a rather sozzled Sloane ranger, managed to stop the car before it crashed into us. Once stopped, the driver literally fell out of the driver's door a bit like Joanna Lumley in an episode of Absolutely

Fabulous. That's when she joined us at the local factory.

The DPG, albeit being work of a mundane and boring nature, was a good posting, and after 14 months of plundering the pot of gold, I was now debt-free with sufficient savings in the bank to put down as a deposit for a house. I had been thinking about returning to the real world for a month or two prior to my posting on Ranger 500 had re-ignited my enthusiasm for real police work. My annual appraisal was due in September, so I took the opportunity to request a transfer back to Tower Bridge. My DPG colleagues considered me a turncoat for wanting to jump ship and work with a new crew sailing under a different captain. It was during my appraisal. I learnt another big word I didn't know the meaning of 'loquatious' – it should have been spelt 'loquacious,' so even the inspector was not that well versed in the written word. The word means talkative, so why not just say that? Either way, that word now joined penultimate into my memory bank for future reference.

A few weeks later, I returned to Tower Bridge, becoming PC593 'M' in the process.

---ooo0ooo---

Chapter 35

Tower Bridge

<u>1980 - 1982</u>

The return

After a sabbatical of 14 months, I returned to Tower Bridge, where apart from a few new faces, very little had changed from when I had left it. One big difference was I went back to work on 'B' relief with a new set of work colleagues, many of whom I had met during relief changeovers during my initial posting.

This time around, I had a good knowledge of the ground, was a police standard driver, and after a brief introduction to the team, I pretty much hit the ground running, being posted straight away to drive either Panda 1 or 2. There was a lack of driving courses coming through to the reliefs, which were now short of qualified drivers. Prior to my arrival, 'B' relief had two advanced drivers, Len and Peter, as well as a standard car driver known affectionately as Griefy. This lack of drivers meant I would pretty much be driving a panda car all the time for the first few months.

Communication between officers and the station was via a personal radio which you signed out when coming on duty. Now personal radios and Griefy never went well together; why that should be, I don't know. Perhaps Griefy was just born unlucky because he would always manage to book out the one personal radio that never seemed to work properly. The reserve room radio had the talk through facility on as a matter of course, so that we were all able to hear and talk to each other. The reserve officer would call for a unit by their number to attend some type of routine work, such as a collapse behind front doors, a personal injury accident, or attend a venue to report a crime. Whenever Griefy's number was called, his radio always seemed to malfunction. The reserve was coming through as clear as a bell calling Griefy to attend an incident; that is when Griefy would answer something like, "Y y y y y y y y y…your…b b b b b b b…breaking…uuuuup,' or 'c c c c c c…can't…h h h h h…hear…y y y y…you.' Now, Griefy appeared to have selective hearing as he couldn't hear any incoming calls, but when he needed to transmit and receive information on a car or a person's details, he came through as clear as a bell. You may well feel that perhaps Griefy was just born unlucky or that he cocked a deaf ear to calls; either way, I enjoyed dealing with anything and everything as it got me back into the mentality of dealing with people.

Police drivers are trained to drive to a relatively high standard. The basic response course included some fast speed driving, and although generally driving to the Highway Code speed limits, we were trained to drive safe but fast in an emergency situation. One emergency situation occurred one Sunday late turn, during which my driving skills were well and truly put to the test in a fast drive to take a patient to the hospital for emergency treatment.

It all began after being paraded and posted to drive Panda 1. I checked the vehicle before driving out of the station yard. Literally, as I did that, a call over the personal radio from a probationer PC requesting assistance to stop a motor vehicle that had committed some type of moving traffic offence. The timing, they say, is everything, and it just so happened that I found myself following right behind the vehicle which I stopped in the Jamaica Road dual carriageway just before the traffic lights with Abbey Street next to a block of flats called Wade House. With the vehicle stopped, I got out and spoke to the driver, explaining that the now hot-footing PC who had come into view wanted to have a word with him. When he arrived, I started to go back to my panda when a man came running from a ground floor flat in Wade House shouting words to the effect, 'my baby has stopped breathing. Behind the man came a woman carrying a baby wrapped in swaddling blankets.

It didn't take a brain surgeon to realise this was a serious life-threatening situation, so shouting over to my colleague, he realised something was amiss and let the errant driver off with a quick warning before coming over to join me. Both the man and woman were now with me, and I could see sure enough the baby was not breathing. I took the baby from the mother and gave her to my colleague, who started using his finger compressions to stimulate the baby's heart, as we all got into the police panda. Whilst doing this, I contacted the station reserve.

"Mike Tango, Mike Tango from 593 - active message...."

"593 go ahead."

"Mike Tango, contact Guys Hospital accident and emergency and inform them I am bringing in a one-week-old baby who has stopped breathing. ETA four minutes."

That's when I started the drive for life. Three traffic lights separated me from my goal: Guys Hospital A&E, and every one of them was against me. The first red was the Jamaica Road - Abbey Street junction, the second Druid Street at the junction with Tower Bridge Road and the third Crucifix Lane at the junction with Bermondsey Street, after which it was pretty much a straight road into the accident and emergency department at Guys Hospital where a group of nursing staff were outside waiting for us, who took the baby from us. The nurses were followed into the hospital by the parents, who understandably seemed to be in a state of shock - whether that was from my driving or the baby's condition, I wouldn't like to say. What I can say is that the total time taken from first being notified by the father to attending the hospital was less than four minutes. We left the child and parents with the nursing staff and went back to patrol. I believe the child made a full recovery – again, job done!

There is no doubt that lady luck was shining that day, firstly on the motorist who got told off rather than prosecuted, and especially on the one-week-old baby and its family. Everything seemed, for whatever reason, to click into place when needed. Driving fast with members of the public on board is not something that I'd advocate unless it is absolutely necessary.

I know of at least one police car accident in which a lost foreign national was being taken back to their hotel as a goodwill gesture. Sod's law, en route, an urgent assistance call came out over the main set that the police driver responded to along with the passenger in the back. During the journey, a wheel came off (literally), and the vehicle crashed, whereby the passenger suffered a serious injury. That caused a lot of writing and years to sort out.

After a couple of months of solid panda driving, my duties changed to alternating between being the operator on 'Mike 2,' the station response car, or driving the station panda. Whenever I was the operator on 'Mike 2,' my driver was mainly Len, the police federation station representative. Len was a thief-taker through and through, and the locals knew him well. Len was held in such esteem by the locals they had nicknamed him 'the screaming skull' and even started painting 'screaming skull' graffiti on walls around the ground. It would be fair to say we had some pretty savoury names we referred to them by, although these seem to have faded in the mists of time—probably the best place for them. The tours we shared were to be eventful, to say the least.

---ooo0ooo---

Chapter 36

Overdose or No Overdose

One of the first incidents Len and I responded to was to a female threatening to jump out of a 2nd-floor maisonette window into the forecourt of the Tyres Estate off Snowfields SE1. On arrival, we found a crowd had gathered around the forecourt area, which is where the female, now clearly visible on an outside windowsill, would land should she indeed decide to jump. Not a good place to stand, so we moved the crowd back a short distance – just in case.

Now our 'would-be jumper' was a rather large breasted female who was sat on the windowsill precariously holding onto a wall-mounted metal waste pipe whilst mumbling over and over to herself. What she was saying only she knew—it was certainly not a language I had ever heard. This was clearly a serious situation as our 'would be jumper' was about 40 feet above the ground, with at best a drop of 14 or so feet onto a meter wide access balcony. To fall 14 feet onto the balcony was bad enough, but assuming she missed that, the next stop was the ground; a fall that she was in all probability not going to survive.

After clearing the landing zone, Len and I went up to the balcony and slowly made our way into the house. The windowsill she was sitting on was her bedroom window, so we went up to her bedroom to talk to her. On entering the room, we could see the 'would be jumper' on the windowsill as well as an empty pill bottle lying on the floor. We never took the Dirty Harry approach of handcuffing her to one of us and telling her to jump—that just didn't cut it. This was a case of slowly edging forwards whilst talking to her. It was pretty much a one-way conversation, but we got close enough to grab both arms and pull her back into the bedroom and onto the floor. Once there she lay immobile whilst every so often giving off an incoherent mumbling sound. Something was amiss, and it seemed to us that she appeared to lapse into and out of consciousness. With that in mind we placed her into the recovery position and called the ambulance service.

The million-dollar question now was, 'Had she taken any of the contents from the pill bottle, and if so, how many?' Try as we might to get her to speak, all we managed to get from her was a mumbled reply that meant the square route of zero. The ambulance crew arrived, and we relayed the circumstances of what had happened to them. We had done our bit; now, it was over to them, so we stood by watching and ready to assist them if need be.

The ambulance crew went about their work checking her vital signs and could find no cause for alarm. Despite this, the female seemed to be getting more and more unresponsive, which perplexed them both initially until one of them decided to check her response levels. To do this, he lifted one of her arms up above her face and promptly dropped it. By rights, the arm should have hit her fair and square in the face, but miraculously, her arm fell to the side, hitting the floor. Maybe that was a fluke, so he tried it again three times, and on every occasion, it did exactly the same thing, falling to the floor alongside her face. With some authority, the ambulance man said, "She's feigning injury, but just to be sure.' And with that, he pulled his right arm sleeve up to the shoulder, after which, he lifted up her top, stuck the palm of his hand between both her breasts, and started to gyrate them both at a fast pace from side to side.

Like two competing jelly moulds, her breasts wobbled from side to side, seeming to travel in separate directions back and forth, slapping against each other in the process before wobbling away again. I could almost imagine him saying 'wahey' and 'lovely, jubbly' as the ambulance man went about the task of vigorously wobbling the fleshy bits backwards and forwards to such an extent that you could hear the *slap, slap* as they moved from side to side. It would be fair to say that Len and I stood mesmerised; it was as if time had stood still. It was certainly not a first-aid move either of us had been trained in, although it's something I suspect we would have enjoyed doing – a manoeuvre that would certainly make the first aid course more interesting, especially for the guys.

So, back to our potential suicide candidate, with her breasts swaying from side to side, she not surprisingly made a miracle recovery to such an extent that she suddenly managed to stand up unaided and, albeit a little red-faced, start to speak lucidly to the ambulance men. We left the ambulance crew to sort the girl out, and our job was done; with smiles on our faces that stretched from ear to ear, we returned to our car and resumed patrol.

---oooOooo---

Chapter 37

Murder most foul

One of the most bizarre investigations Len and I were called upon to investigate involved an allegation of such cruelty that it literally left the victim hung, drawn and quartered Using all our skill and training we successfully identified the culprit, he was caught bang to rights and didn't have a leg to stand on.

It all started when we responded to an emergency call from IR (Information Room) to attend a venue on the Astley Cooper Estate and speak to a distraught female informant.

The information was a bit sketchy, so we responded using the blues and twos and got to the informant post-haste, where we attended the informant's house and knocked on the door. The front door opened, and we were greeted by our informant, a rotund lady wearing a negligee at least three sizes or more too small into which she had somehow managed to pour her body. Least ways that was my take on it. Our informant was indeed well endowed, and though attempting to maintain her modesty, failed dismally as the negligee she was wearing was sheer and mainly see through. It must have been made of some high-grade material to withstand the 'G' forces it was now being subjected to. That said, it looked to us like it was beginning to lose the struggle to hold back the mounting pressure.

In particular, clearly visible at the neck was a single button being kept under constant tension. It was held in place by an inch or so length of needle thread which was close to losing the will to live. That button sent me into a trance, and I started thinking, *what if that thread suddenly gave up the ghost propelling the button off at one of us like a bullet being fired from a gun?* The big question was which one of us was going to get hit by it. Sod's law meant it could hit either one of us in a vulnerable place, such as an eye. If that happened it could end up with one or both of us both ending up in hospital. All the time my thoughts were going over possible problems, such as how would we explain to our wives or fellow relief members that we had been shot by a missile discharged from a woman's negligee? We would have had been the laughing stock of the station for sure.

Luckily, that never happened as the trance was broken after a few seconds when she spoke up and invited us into the front room. Once there, we stood as she sat down on a settee alongside several young children. When settled, she told us the gory details.

The informant had cogitated for a few hours over whether to call the police, finally deciding to do so when her conscience got the better of her, and so, she dialled 999. The saga started some three or four hours earlier when a number of wild ducks had landed on top of some garage/shed roofs within the estate road. Someone had taken a pot shot at one of the ducks with an air rifle, and I guess more by luck than judgment had actually managed to hit one, killing it stone dead. Our informant did not know who fired the shot, but she did know that the dead duck had been recovered from the shed roof by a nearby neighbour who she believed had taken it home. Now our informant knew the neighbour by sight although did not know the flat where they lived— that was something we would have to find out. Law-abiding she might be, but she was not willing to make a witness statement and definitely would not attend court to give evidence. In fact, as far as she was concerned by telling us, she had more than done her civic duty. So, having got it off her chest, the ball was now in our court to deal with. That's when she showed us the door, and we left her still wearing her fully loaded negligee with a primed exploding button luckily still in place. Phew, that was a close call.

Now safely out of harm's way, we trundled off to find the dastardly dead duck plunderer. Using every ounce of our combined investigative skills; by that, I mean walking along with the balcony and looking through a few kitchen windows we came across a kitchen full of duck feathers either lying on the furniture or floating around in the air almost as if a feather pillow had just exploded. Sat in the middle of the kitchen table in a large pan where the bones and dismembered carcass of a bird. Bingo, making an educated guess, we reckoned we had found the lair of the dead duck plunderer, so we knocked on the door, which was opened by an out of work young man with fat still visible around his face. It didn't take us long to crack our suspect who readily admitted recovering the duck to eat it after it had been shot by someone else. Who that someone else was he said he did not know? Did I believe him? No. He probably did know that and may even have been the shooter, but we had no evidence to prove otherwise.

He had to be seriously hungry to do this as it meant removing the duck's feathers and guts and preparing it for cooking. I mentally gave him an 'A' for effort on that because, in truth, this was no mean feat. Even though this was not the type of action we would want to promulgate, neither of us felt there was sufficient evidence to affect an arrest for essentially eating a dead duck. We decided to ruffle his feathers a bit and told him he had committed the crime of eating a 'queen's duck' (a crime we had just made up), whereupon we read him his fortune. After this, Len and I left him and went about our business.

This was just another day in the life of an everyday police officer looking at death (well, maybe the remains of something dead on this occasion). Either way, the feathers and the leftovers were not a pretty sight.

---ooo0ooo---

Chapter 38

Drunks never learn

One night duty, Len and I were manning Mike 2 when a call came out to a serious disturbance at a pub in Deptford. Along with a number of other units, we responded and arrived in time to see a dog handler dealing with a group of six drunks whom he had told to move away. One of them, who I will call 'Mouthy,' was being a complete pain in the proverbial, continually arguing and threatening the officer. Now, these were not the normal group of drunken young males so often seen; they were three couples, all in their thirties, who seemed to fit more into the 'yuppie' scene.

Now an unwritten rule I tend to follow is not to intervene when another officer is dealing with a situation unless asked to do so or the situation requires it. The hackles at the back of my neck were slowly rising, and my heart rate noticeably quickened when the dog handler left them and walked away, with 'Mouthy' still giving it large. Now leaving someone in these circumstances can cause a problem for other officers at some future date. So, with that in mind, I went over and said to all of them, "You've had a good drink; you are all drunk, so go home and sleep it off." Now, to their credit, five of them were no problem giving it the standard "Yes, officer; we are all going home now" reply. It was no surprise to me that Mouthy wanted to take it further.

"Do you know who I am?" said Mouthy, to which I replied, "Sure; sign your drunk when you can't remember your name. Now do yourself a favour and go home with your friends." An olive branch had been offered to Mouthy for him to go home and sleep off the effects of drink; an option that had it been taken would probably see him suffering nothing more than a bit of a headache in the morning. Unfortunately for him, he was 'disinclined to acquiesce' to that course of action, retorting with a few loud expletives that I considered to be disorderly behaviour. Now, enough is enough, and having suffered enough of his diatribe, I arrested him for being 'drunk and disorderly.'

Mouthy was giving it large in the back of the police van as we went back to the station saying words to the effect of "You have no idea who you are dealing with" and "I'll make you pay for this insult." What Mouthy did not know was that he had won the mystery first prize of a free, all-inclusive one-day holiday that started with a police car ride to Tower Bridge Police Station. Once there, Mouthy would sign in at the reception and be shown to his en suite hotel room. To ensure he enjoyed his stay, I placed him into Cell 1, the station's first-class accommodation for numbskulls. I suspect that if asked, Mouthy would have agreed with our five-star accommodation rating.

Sometime during the night, Mouthy was charged with being drunk and disorderly and kept in until the morning when after a full English breakfast on cardboard plates with plastic cutlery had been provided, Mouthy was taken before the Tower Bridge Magistrates where payback would be dished out. So, he found himself taken over to the court and placed in the cell with other drunks awaiting 10:00 a.m., the witching hour when he would appear bedraggled in front of the magistrate. Mouthy pleaded not guilty, and the case was remanded to another date for the matter to be heard.

Now, being drunk and disorderly is a purely summary case that is heard before magistrates, either lay or stipendiary. On this occasion, it was to be heard before a stipendiary magistrate. With Mouthy standing in the dock, I entered when called and gave my evidence, and with no questions asked or challenges made to my evidence, it meant Len's evidence was simply tendered. With our case now complete, it was Mouthy's turn to give evidence. Not surprisingly, the other five persons present when this incident occurred all declined to attend court in his defence. I guess that pretty much gives an insight into his obnoxious and odious personality. So now, Mouthy gave evidence from the witness box where he admitted having had a drink, although he was certainly not drunk. That's when he pointed to me and said, "That officer told me to F--- Off." *Would I say something like that*...either way, it was academic as the magistrate replied, "So, why didn't you F--- Off?"

Mouthy was unable to answer that question—the case was proved and he was fined the princely sum of £25. So, for being a complete arse, Mouthy had suffered the humiliation of an overnight stay in police cells, lost two days' pay, and been fined the princely sum of £25 to boot. As for Len and I, we both incurred overtime for attending court. Oh, and I'm still waiting for Mouthy to make me pay for arresting him. Somehow, I don't think that is going to happen.

Another disturbance call Len and I responded to one night during the relief changeover was at the Dun Cow public house. The Dun Cow public house was a large establishment strategically placed on the corner of the Old Kent Road and Dunton Road. (it's now a doctor's surgery).

On our arrival, the area outside the pub was heaving with customers exiting through a number of side doors. Bam Bam, still wearing his big beaming grin, was standing in the road with other police officers marshalling the customers away. It was whilst he was doing this that one of the customers decided it was a good idea to suddenly punch Bam Bam full in the face. Now, Bam Bam was built a bit like 'Odd Job,' the villain from the James Bond's *'Goldfinger.'*. Bam Bam's stature and the fact he was a Met Police 1st team rugby player meant he was as hard as nails.

It was no surprise then that Bam Bam never flinched and, in fact, was still grinning following the unprovoked attack. What someone thought was a good idea at the time was, in the cold light of day, a decidedly bad idea. The errant individual was not smiling when Bam Bam responded in kind, and like Mouthy, he was lucky enough to win a free, all-inclusive one-day holiday to the police station and endure the same high standard of customer service reserved for special clients. This individual also won the booby prize of having his photograph and fingerprints taken and being allocated a unique CRO number that would remain with him for life.

Drink was the common denominator that changed the way people behaved. Disturbance calls to pubs and parties on night duty were as numerous as fleas on a dog. Drinking made (still make) people unpredictable, so you learnt to take extra care with them.

---ooo0ooo---

Chapter 39

Money, Money, Money!

I had heard of the musician Jethro Tull but had never heard of the name Allan Tull until one Saturday when I was again riding shotgun with Len in Mike 2. We had just left the station to resume our patrol following our one-hour breakfast break. I seem to recall I was bellyaching about being subjected to a humiliatingly one-sided game of snooker where I had scored a measly 5 to Lens 55. It was obviously an in-depth discussion that left Len grinning like the proverbial Cheshire cat. Our banter was suddenly interrupted by a call from Information Room (IR), which went a bit like this:

"Any wireless car on M Division able to assist a Central unit requesting uniform assistance."

I answered, "M2 MP. Mike 2 is able to assist."

"Mike 2, thank you. Change to radio channel 54 and call Central 123 for details."

"M2 MP, changing now," and with that, I changed channels as requested and called Central 123.

A meet was arranged on Carter Streets patch somewhere in the Rodney Road area just off the New Kent Road. This was Mike 3's ground, but as they had not answered, we left our patch and went to poach on theirs. Arriving at our assigned location, we spoke to the Detective Inspector (DI) from the South East Regional Crime Squad (SERCS). The DI said he was in charge of an ongoing operation but was careful not to discuss it in any great detail. What he did say went a bit like this.

"Right, gents, I want you to stop a Rolls Royce that is currently being followed by our surveillance team. There may be a small parcel under the passenger's seat, and if you are not satisfied with his possession of it, please feel free to arrest him."

We were some distance away from the vehicle by this time, but with blues and twos, we cut through the Saturday traffic like a knife through butter, making ground on the surveillance team that was providing a running commentary keeping us updated on the vehicle's position—along Thurlow Street, left into Albany Road, into Shorncliffe Road, right onto the Old Kent Road, left into Rowcross Street, and right into Rolls Road. The surveillance team peeled away as we came up behind the Rolls Royce in Rolls Road roughly midway along the road's length. We flashed our blue light and indicated for the vehicle to stop, which it did. Ironically, the location where the vehicle had been stopped was now on Tower Bridge's manner, so we were no longer poaching on Carter Street's ground. I went over to the driver, Alan Tull, and explained the reason for the stop. I asked him to get out of the vehicle, which is when Len joined us.

Asking a few cursory questions, we found out the vehicle was not owned by him. I think he said it belonged to his mother. With no proof of identity, a search was made of the cars interior—in particular, under the front passenger seat was made. Nothing even faintly resembling a small parcel was visible, and I was beginning to feel this would just be a stop where the driver's details would later be passed over to the SERCS officers. After the interior had been searched, Len said to Tull, "Is there anything in the boot?" He replied something like "dirty washing."

Walking around to the car boot, Len opened it up, and the only thing I recall seeing in it was a large brown beige leather suitcase with side straps that was lying flat on the boot floor. It was nothing extraordinary, just a medium-sized suitcase that conceivably could have contained dirty washing. Allan was pretty unfazed by having been stopped by us, and I detected no readily identifiable outward signs of apprehension or stress even when Len was about to open the suitcase. The suitcase contents were not dirty laundry, but it was certainly going to an illegal laundry somewhere because it was stuffed wall to wall with counterfeit money. You may wonder how we were able to say so quickly that the suitcase contained counterfeit money.

That's because there were thousands of sheets of A2 paper, each sheet of which contained about 25 individual prints of counterfeit £20 notes (something like £500 a sheet) that had not yet been cut down into individual note sizes. Once cut down, it was destined for use as money within the local economy. At a guess, the potential street value of the notes in this suitcase was somewhere in the region of £1,000,000. Money can do funny things to people. In this instance, it changed Len into a super-fast copper. I'd never seen him move so fast; as quick as a flash, he dropped the suitcase lid, turned, grabbed Allan Tull's hands, and in one breath arrested and cautioned him. Allan Tull was still unfazed by this sudden turn of events and just held both wrists out, waiting quietly until Len applied a set of high-quality police bracelets. Once secured, Allan was placed in the back of Mike 2.

Central 123 was immediately notified, and we were directed to take the vehicle and prisoner immediately to Catford Police Station, which is exactly what we did. Allan was booked in, our arrest notes and witness statements were completed, and the three exhibits of the car key, the car, and the suitcase and its counterfeit notes contents were exhibited and produced in line with court requirements. Other SERC team members were now busy executing a number of search warrants that resulted in the arrest of many more team members along with additional seizures of counterfeit notes in excess of 20 million pounds, a printing press and a few firearms to boot.

It goes without saying that as we were in the canteen, we had another game of snooker where I was fleeced again by Len. *When would I learn?* Game completed; we left our original arrest notes and statements with the designated interview officers and returned to Tower Bridge to resume our patrol. It would be fair to say we had a Cheshire cat-sized smile on our faces. As for Allan, his winning ticket would see him having a much longer all expenses paid holiday than was the norm. I think his was a jackpot ticket.

The next time I saw him again was in the dock at the Central Criminal Court Old Bailey along with a number of co-defendants when I was called to give evidence on the first day of the trial. The court case was a bit bizarre as the trial judge was a Queen's Counsel (QC) sitting as a judge, the prosecution was conducted by Senior Treasury Counsel (TC) (the equivalent of a QC), and each defendant (of which there were now eight) was represented by their own QC. Now, a QC is entitled to have a junior counsel (a less experienced barrister) to assist him, and so, it was that the QC's each had their own junior counsel.

To say the court was crowded would be an understatement as apart from the trial judge, there were a total of eighteen barristers sitting in their section of the court packed together like sardines in a tin. Entering into this arena was PC 593M Glenister, where after swearing the oath and introducing myself to the court, I gave my evidence in Chief. The prosecuting barristers led me through the circumstances that led to the seizure of the property recovered and Allan Tull's arrest, pausing for effect at salient parts. When I got to the suitcase exhibit, LS/3 Treasury Council asked for it to be passed up to me in the witness box. I was surprised that the ushers could even pick the case up, but despite the weight, that's exactly what two of them did, bringing it up to me in the witness box.

Treasury Counsel went on. "Is that the suitcase you recovered from the Rolls Royce?" I examined the exhibit label and, after seeing my signature on it, said 'yes'.

Treasury Counsel said, "Can you open it up and show the contents to the jury please," which is exactly what I did. When the contents were shown, there was a tangible intake of breath from all those present, including all the jury members, which was followed a short while later with a few "oohs." and "aahs." similar to the sound made by the "Minions" in the Despicable Me films.

All of the defendant's sixteen barristers could have asked questions of me in cross-examination, although in reality, only those representing Allan Tull did so. The evidence I gave was not really contested in any great detail. I found it quite bizarre to stand in the witness box after being cross-examined by one barrister for each of the other barristers to stand up in turn and say "no questions" before sitting down again, a bit like the Mexican wave at a football match.

My bit was done; I was released from the court, and the case continued. As for Allan, he was later convicted of a number of offences and, I believe, received an eight-year sentence. So, his winning holiday ticket was indeed a jackpot winner reserved for auspicious customers.

---ooo0ooo---

Chapter 40

Vehicle Chases

As a youngster, I watched the car chases in programs such as "The Sweeney," and wished I could be there with them when they laid hands upon the baddies when they either crashed or abandoned their vehicles and tried to run away. Now, as a police driver, I, at last, had an opportunity to get behind a lost or stolen and live the dream. Luckily, car chases were a regular occurrence that seemed to happen when you least expected it. I cannot explain the high you get from the adrenaline rush the moment you picked up a vehicle refusing to stop and started to relay a running commentary over the radio.

With Len in Mike 2, we enjoyed a few vehicle chases, each one resulting in a collar. One vehicle chase, we had involved a Norton 750 Commando motorbike which, by all rights, we never had a hope in hells chance of catching. Luckily for us, the bike rider was anything but competent, and that gave us the edge.

It all started when we were minding our business during one night duty when we turned left from Tower Bridge Road onto the Old Kent Road via the Bricklayers Arms slip road. Just as we approached the Old Kent Road at its junction with the Bricklayers Road overpass, what should appear over the horizon travelling at a very fast speed was none other than a Norton 750 Commando motorbike being ridden by a single rider. The rider, for good measure, was driving a bit erratically in the process doing a bit of zig-zagging job in between the traffic. It was effectively a call to arms, and with a "he'll do." from Len, who did no more than putting the pedal to the floor and shot off after the motorbike; for effect, the blues and twos kicked in to wake those about to sleep. Needless to say, Chummy had no intention of stopping for us as he continued on along the Old Kent Road, in and out of traffic and ignoring a number of red traffic lights in the process. I was straight on the main set to Information Room (IR), saying "M2 MP – Mike 2 active message – chase Old Kent Road towards Deptford."

Back came the reply "Mike 2 – Go ahead." With permission granted, I gave the running commentary in clipped updates that allowed other nearby police wireless cars such as Papa 7, Mike 4, and a few others to start making their way in our direction to take up the chase if need be. In truth, I expected Chummy to turn around and give us the universal middle finger salute before twisting the throttle and disappearing into the sunset. Luckily for us, that never happened mainly due to the fact that Chummy seemed to be having some difficulty of his own controlling the bike, which would suddenly speed up and begin to draw away from us before suddenly slowing down again. Chummy continued along the Old Kent Road, still weaving in and out of traffic as he did so and by now had reached the St. James Road traffic lights, which is when Chummy suddenly decided to turn left off the Old Kent Road in St. James Road. We turned into St. James Road a few seconds later to see him and the bike wobbling a bit as he attempted to negotiate a bend into Rotherhithe New Road. That's when it all went pear-shaped for Chummy as a parting of the way occurred that saw his motorbike go one way whilst he went the other, zooming along the ground pretty much using the seat of his leather trousers as a sledge, missing all the other traffic in the process before coming to an abrupt stop in the middle of the road splayed out on his back. Len stopped Mike 2 safely, and we ran over to see what was left of Chummy. Having expected the worse, I was surprised to find that apart from a hole in his leather trouser seat through which a red buttock now glowed, Chummy had not suffered any injury that needed treating in hospital. A result for sure, as otherwise we would have been tied up waiting for him to be seen instead of sheeting him at the station. It was no surprise that Chummy was arrested for driving whilst unfit, taken to the police station and after being booked in searched. During that search, a small amount of "wacky baccy." in a resin lump was found in his wallet. End result: Chummy was charged with a number of driving offences, as well as possession of drugs, was sent in custody to court, pleaded guilty whereupon the court disqualified him from driving and fined him accordingly. Job done.

On another night-duty tour, Len and I had just left the factory in Rotherhithe, heading along Lower Road towards the Surrey Docks one way system when an Austin 1100 took a corner on two wheels directly in front of us. Now it was the first shift of our seven-night posting, which can leave you a bit jaded in the recognition department, but it didn't take a brain surgeon to realise this type of driving was going to grab our attention. So, to the sound of "Tally Ho," the chase began. We never turned the flashing blue lights on until Len got up right behind it, which is when we knew for sure the driver wasn't going to stop as he accelerated away. That's when the full package of flashing blue light followed by the noise of the two-tone horns split the night asunder. Straight on the radio to IR, with a running commentary that IR kept for posterity on audiotapes, the pursuit was broadcast over the main set. The main set came alive with backup vehicles, basically bored wireless car drivers who took the opportunity to hone their skills with a bit of fast blues and two's driving, all now zeroing into our location to back us up if needed. The vehicle was not shown as having been lost or stolen, although if it had only just been lifted, it would be too early for any report of that nature to have been filed.

The chase went around the Surrey Docks one way system, back to our original location before it went into the one-way system again and suddenly turned left from Lower Road into Redriff Road, speeding along with it until it turned right into Rotherhithe Street where it drove to the very end before turning right into Elgar Street and following the road around into Gulliver Street. It was at this point that the driver started to slow down, and it was pretty obvious that he was looking to decamp from the vehicle into the Odessa Street estate. The mistake he made came when he turned into an estate access road entrance only to find it was blocked by a locked gate. A bit of a problem as this stopped the driver dead in his tracks from going any further, causing him to hit the brakes rather hard, but not hard enough to stop him from hitting the gate and roll back a bit so that his car came to rest with the driver's door now wedged against a gate post that prevented him from opening the door and having it on his dancers.

Undeterred, the driver wound down the driver's door window, placed his hands onto the roof, and literally levered himself through it, whereby he ungainly slumped to the floor, before picking himself up and running off into the estate, followed by yours truly. Len was now giving a situation update before following in my footsteps to back me up. Luckily Len never had to run too far as I caught Chummy pretty quickly, and he was now well and truly restrained. I walked him back to the car he had just crashed, which is where I again joined Len. Needless to say, Chummy, now secured in an arm lock, was not a happy bunny at having been caught.

Chummy was taken to Tower Bridge, where he admitted to stealing the car. Unfortunately for him, enquiries revealed the car had been the proud possession of a man who had passed away two days before, and the deceased's next of kin were not best pleased that their loved one's pride and joy was now a damaged heap. As next of kin, they willingly provided a loser's statement and, armed with that, Chummy was charged and sent in custody to be dealt with at court the next day, where I would present the case before the magistrates.

It was whilst I was in court waiting for this case to be called that Rubberbum entered the courtroom door and walked across a strangely quiet court on a pair of shoes that continually emitted an "eeking" sound. Over to the list officer, he went *eek, eek, eek, eek, eek* as he did so. After a brief conversation with the court officer, Rubberbum returned the way he had come *eek, eek, eek, eek, eeking*, leaving the court through the custody area doors. Rubberbum was oblivious to the fact that the eeking noise from his shoes had caused both the magistrate and "Giss," the court sergeant, to stop what they were doing and just stare after Rubberbum as he exited the court.

My defendant was brought into the court, and I went into the witness box to ask for the offences to be put. As the offences were about to be put, Rubberbum decided to make another court appearance as he *eek. eek, eek, eeked* from the custody area back over to the poor old court officer a distance of about ten feet. He never made it because as soon as the "eeking" started, "Giss," the court sergeant, moving faster than I had ever thought he was capable of, grabbed hold of Rubberbum and physically swung him back into the custody area through the same door he had just entered by. There were a few suppressed smiles from those in the court, and it took a minute or so after that that the court clerk had composed himself sufficiently to put the charges to my prisoner who pleaded guilty after each charge was readout. With the magistrate telling the prisoner to sit down, I gave details of the offence, adding for good measure a bit about the distress this had caused to the deceased next of kin - a sort of early version of a victim's impact statement now standard across the court system. Clearly not impressed, the magistrate gave my prisoner a three-month lie-down. Job done.

My third chase occurred when one night duty, I was driving an unmarked Hillman Hunter police car with Griefy riding shotgun as my front seat passenger. Lightening, as it is said, does not normally strike twice, but speaking from experience, I can say it obviously does. We were paired up working a bank holiday; that meant we were earning overtime being paid at double time. Our sergeants had informed us during our briefing that apart from the eight hours guaranteed for working a bank holiday, under no circumstances was any additional overtime to be incurred. Perhaps not a wise decision in the circumstances to post Griefy and I together.

Changes were ever-present in the police, and now with driving accidents on the increase, changes were being made to police cars in an effort to improve driver safety. The change that some brain surgeons had come up with was that only the area cars, station vans, and duty officers' vehicles should have main set radios installed in them. All other vehicles were not to respond to emergency calls. This should lead to fewer cars responding to calls. Which in turn meant fewer vehicles driving fast and, ergo fewer accidents. That did not take into account the fact that whatever came over the Main Set radio was then relayed via the wireless operator to other mobile units over the station's personal radio. The end result of this decision was the removal of a number of main set radios from police panda cars and other unmarked vehicles. Communication was poor to start with, and this decision just exacerbated the situation. It was no surprise that my vehicle was one of those that had had the main set radio removed, leaving a jumble of loose wires where it had been fitted.

With only our personal radios as our communication method, we went out on patrol. The drawback to only having a personal radio was their lack of distance over which they transmitted and, in some cases, even black spots where they never worked at all. All night long, Griefy and I put ourselves about, but we found nothing untoward to whet our appetite, or more to the point, 'make someone's day.' That's when we depressingly returned to the station and took our refreshments. Now fully charged, when Mike 2 came in for their refreshments, we left and resumed our patrol again. Again, minding our own business, we chewed the fat over some recent hot topic, slowly driving along the Lower Road when a vehicle came out of Redriff Road into the Surrey Docks one way system. It came out so fast that it almost hit us side-on in the process. Was this Deja Vu or what? The only difference was the car was travelling in the opposite direction to the one I had chased previously. Again, it wasn't rocket science that led us to believe it was a lost or stolen vehicle, and sure enough, the driver didn't disappoint us as he decided to ignore my request to stop putting his "metal to the pedal" as he accelerated away with us now in pursuit. There it was again: "Tally Ho," and off we went.

Griefy started giving the commentary over the personal radio (strange that on this occasion, he had picked a radio that worked). The Mike 2 crew left their food in the canteen at Tower Bridge and, to their credit, made their way towards us. That was a big ask as they had to make up three or four miles before they would be in a position to take over.

Personal radios per se were a bit of a problem as they had limited transmission range and were prone to communication black spots where they didn't work at all. It didn't help that the Surrey Docks one way system was right on the edge of our ground. We were now committed to chasing the vehicle, which sped off towards Greenwich, getting ever further away from our base station—a process that increased the range and reduced the communication quality. This was when we needed the main set as we sped along Evelyn Street and Creek Road and into the Greenwich one way system.

With Mike 2 now running towards us, the operator had got straight onto the main set and informed Information Room (IR) of our chase, and IR, in turn, linked the station radio channel into the main set channel—a procedure which thankfully for us had the effect of extending our transmission coverage. Wireless cars from across the area acknowledged and rushed to join in the chase that had now exited the Greenwich one way system and was now speeding along Trafalgar Road into the roundabout with the A2 flyover. There, it went straight on into Woolwich Road passing Makro's in Charlton towards Woolwich. Effectively, we were travelling fast but in a straight line on a road that thankfully had only light traffic on it. Papa 7 was soon coming up fast behind us, vying with Romeo 4 to become the lead vehicle and take over the chase. The driving hierarchy decreed that response cars were obliged to give way to a wireless response car when they were in a position to safely do so. With my dander now up, it went against my instinct to do that. This was especially so when IR started telling me that when the wireless cars were in a position to do so, I was to let them take over the chase. Communication is everything, and strangely, that's when Griefy came into his own. At first hand, I heard him start speaking into the personal radio something I had heard many times before as manipulating the switch as he started with the now-familiar "'Y…y-y-y-y…you're…b-b-b…b-b-breaking up IR…r-r-r…repeat."

It was only a delaying tactic, but it kept us as the lead car in the chase for a little longer than otherwise. This was just as well because just then the bandit car driver clipped a roadside kerb, causing the vehicle to spin 180 degrees so that the bandit car driver was now going backwards out of control at a fast rate of knots. The chase was now effectively over, and the driver was going nowhere fast, so I braked sharply to increase the gap between us, luckily just in time as the back wheels hit the kerbstones again so hard that the car tyres shredded, causing the bandit vehicle to come to an abrupt stop in the middle of the road somewhere near Hardens Manorway.

That's where we were joined by all and sundry, including Mike 2, who had had an amazing drive to make up so much ground so fast. Despite all the blue flashing lights everywhere, Griefy and I ran over and made certain that the collar was ours. The driver was a juvenile recidivist (someone that continually re-offends) who we took back to Woolwich Police Station and processed. As a recidivist, the duty officer authorised his immediate charge and arrangements were made for him to appear before the next sitting juvenile court. What happened to him after that, I don't know, but apart from making my day with a bit of excitement, he also earned me a lot of double bubble over time, which we were obliged to gratefully accept.

Now it may seem that we won every chase, but that was far from reality. Nicky, Jacko, Piddly and the rest of the Four Squares boys were a constant challenge. It seemed that every day one of them would go to a Central London self-serve car park, take the pick of whichever car caught their fancy, jump in and brazen as you like simply drive off in it back to Bermondsey. Once there, they would promptly park up with the engine running somewhere near the Jamaica Road roundabout at the Junction with St. James Road, where they waited to bate a police car into a chase situation. The odds were heavily stacked in their favour as they were driving top of the range Audi Quattro's and Golf GTI's whilst we, for the most part, were driving 1100cc pandas.

The analogy would be to bet on the donkey entering a hurdles race against Red Rum—no contest, really. That was unless you changed the odds in your favour, something that Piddly would find out to his cost a few months later where unbeknown to him, the odds were heavily stacked in the donkey's favour, but that's another story.

---ooo0ooo---

Chapter 41

If you give it you've got to take it

One early turn around 8:30 a.m. Len and I were in Mike 2 travelling along Drummond Road with the four squares estate on our left generally in the direction of Southwark Park Road when travelling towards us from the opposite direction was a white mini clubman estate clearly being driven by a local youth by the name of Russell. Russell was known to us because he associated with a group of local youths who were into anything and everything. Russell was not wanted but for sure should not have been driving since he had no driving licence, car insurance or MOT certificate.

Game on – Spinning Mike 2 around in one movement we hot-footed it back along Drummond Road in the direction we had just come from in time to see the white minivan now parked up on double yellow lines about 10 yards from the junction with Jamaica Road, with Russell the driver now running rather fast along the Jamaica Road pavement eventually disappearing into the flats of the four squares estate. It was to our advantage that Russell, in his haste to get away, had failed to consider where he had parked, in this case on double yellow lines near the main road junction, and what's more, the vehicle engine was still turning over, powered by a makeshift ignition key fashioned from a front door yale key.

I guessed Russell was now playing a waiting game, banking on the fact that we could not wait indefinitely for him to return to the vehicle and that in time we would have to resume our patrol, and as sure as we did that Russell would undoubtedly return to the vehicle and drive away in it. That was something we didn't want to happen – it would never do for Russell to think he had had us over, so as the vehicle was illegally parked and causing obstruction, the solution was for us to relocate the vehicle to a safer location – for argument's sake a police car pound.

Police advanced car drivers are pretty much authorised to drive any vehicle, whilst I was a Class 4 van driver was authorised to drive the wireless car so hey presto a win double just when we needed it. All we needed was official permission to do so, which was granted by Central Traffic Control, who we had called up direct on the wireless cars main set channel. The offending vehicle was to be taken to the Willow Walk car police car pound post haste. We no longer wanted Russell to return to the car, so not waiting for the paint to dry, Len handed over the police car keys to me, and like a greyhound, he went over to the minivan and before you knew it was in the driver's seat and off like a long dog driving away. Yours truly followed behind in Mike 2. Up to the junction with the Jamaica Road, we went, and despite a heavy volume of traffic, we wasted little time in edging out into the nearside lane and slowly started moving towards the Abbey Road roundabout. Everything was going fine until suddenly I looked in the rear-view mirror and saw that Russell had magically re-appeared behind me from the direction of the Four Squares estate and was now running along the pavement towards us accompanied by his friend Paul shouting at the top of his voice "Stop thief." Straight into Jamaica Road, he ran, dodging between cars as he sought to catch up to the slow-moving minivan, appearing to be gaining at every stride until he was running alongside it, hitting the passenger side window as he did so. It was unfortunate for Russell that at that moment, the traffic which had baulked Lens progress suddenly cleared, and he was able to accelerate away in the minivan, leaving an exasperated Russell trailing in his wake. I could almost hear Len heaving a sigh of relief in the knowledge our plan had come good.

So, although Len was gone, I clearly had to stop and deal with Russell, who was, to put it mildly, going through every swear word he could think of, although by far the most common word started with a C that he repeated over and over again. Russell's head was so red I thought it was about to explode; at the very least, he was hopping mad and spitting blood. I stopped Mike 2 by the pavement a little further along Jamaica Road and parked up. It meant Russell had to walk a bit further, which made me feel better.

Clearly, he was upset, so for my part, I slowly got out of the vehicle walked to the pavement removing a process book from my back pocket as I did so.

Then armed with a pen, I turned to deal with Russell.

Now in volatile situations, it's worth remembering the two-minute rule. It's one used very effectively by hot air balloon pilots to appease farmers whose crops they have just trashed during an emergency landing. The rule basically states that no one can be angry for more than two minutes of concerted verbal abuse as, by the end of that time, they have blown themselves out. Try it out – it works. Russell easily was an angry person, and this easily fell into the volatile situation category, so I applied this training with Russell. Pitching my voice low, I remained calm in the face of his continued abuse, during which he uncontrollably shouted, trying to control the situation by trying to talk over me. I did not allow this to happen, and speaking slowly, I went into my process reporting mode, saying, "Russell, I am reporting you for causing unnecessary obstruction and parking your vehicle on double yellow lines. Those are the two reasons your vehicle has been removed to the car pound." That done, I followed it with a caution "You do not have to say anything unless you wish to do so, but anything you say will be taken down in writing and may be given in evidence."

I doubt whether he heard or took in everything I said. What I did discover was that Russell's knowledge of swear words seemed to be limited to the C-word that he continued to shout over and over again. The C-word was the only reply he made to the caution, so I recorded as accurately as I could all the times he shouted the C-word at me; a process that ironically took me about two minutes to complete and strangely sufficient time for Russell to vent his spleen before pretty much running out of steam, eventually stopping altogether just like a balloon imploding. As the expletives stopped, I judged the time right to say, "Okay, Russell; you said a lot, so to make sure that I have recorded your reply accurately, I'm going to repeat it back to you." Your reply to the caution was "You c—ts, a word I repeated twenty times again or so." Do you agree with what I have recorded, or have I missed a few "You c—ts." out. Russell was gobsmacked and unable to reply. So, for good measure, I said, "Would you like to sign this reply as being accurate?"

You can guess by now that Russell was not particularly receptive, although having now calmed down to a rational level, we were able to engage in a more amicable manner. I said, "Russell, you tried it on and came off second best. Your vehicle is at Pages Walk car pound, and you will need to take your driving documents with you and pay the removal fee to get it back; otherwise, it will be scrapped." I left a disconsolate Russell almost in tears on the side of Jamaica

Road with his friend Paul, got back into the driver's seat of Mike 2 and drove to the car pound to pick up Len. When I got to the car pound, Len was laughing like a drain. "Daisy, that was a close call; I never knew he could run so fast. Do you know he hit the passenger window so hard he almost knocked it out of its mountings into my lap? Luckily I was in the mainstream by then accelerating away."

Russell had tried to have one over on the forces of the law – something in which, certainly on this occasion, he came off a poor second. The end result of this episode was that Russell's pride and joy had been taken away from him, stuck in a car pound and was later sold as scrap a few weeks later.

In good old fashioned policing terms, 'quite apart from the satisfaction,' it gave us. An uninsured car was removed from the road, making them safer for other motorists and users. Job done!

You could say Russell received an "experiential learning course" from the University of Life, which is not cheap…well, it wasn't for him.

---ooo0ooo---

Chapter 42

Misper

Missing person reports are dealt with on an individual basis dependent upon a number of factors that include the person's age, the circumstances surrounding the disappearance, and whether they are at risk of harm. It was not unusual for patrol officers to be sent to check an address for the whereabouts of a missing person. I was allocated a missing person enquiry to deal with one late turn when I turned up for work and was posted to drive the station van – call sign Mike Tango 2. This particular missing person enquiry (more commonly referred to as a Misper) related to a 14-year-old girl who had been reported as missing towards the end of the early turn shift. It just so happened that someone from the late turn would have to deal with it, and a bit like pass the parcel when the briefing stopped, it had landed in my cap.

The bottom line was this girl was believed to be staying at a family address in Marcia Road with her boyfriend, Trevor. Trevor was known to me as he had previously come to the notice of the police, with intelligence on record that he was known to be violent. Well violent he may be, but for me to deal with this enquiry, I still needed to attend the address and speak with him. So straight after leaving our briefing, I jumped into the hot seat of Mike Tango 2 and off I went to Marcia Road. A knock on the door was answered by Trevor, and I quickly found out that he was indeed the missing girl's boyfriend, although her current whereabouts were unknown and most definitely not in the address. I had no specific power to demand entry to search Trevor's address. Perhaps, it was my expression of disbelief, or my continued presence in the doorway, that led to him inviting me into the premises, an invitation I readily accepted, immediately entering the house and treating each room to a cursory visual inspection as we passed them in turn.

Sure enough, there was no obvious sign of the missing person being present. So, after having a word with Trevor to the effect if he saw his girlfriend, he was to ask her to contact her parents and the police as soon as possible, I left the premises. Before going back on patrol, I updated the station reserve, adding that unless the contact was made with the girl, further enquiries would be made there later. Off I trundled to deal with other calls as they came in.

Little did I know that my actions that day would set the wheels in motion leading to a complaint being made against me where words of advice were given—given nicely but nonetheless given. So, what brought about this complaint? That all started when I took a call an hour or so later to a flat on the Longfield Estate to speak to a victim, an ex-boyfriend of the missing girl who had just been threatened with serious violence by none other than Trevor. Trevor, the girl's current beau, believed (erroneously as it turned out) that the victim had been the one responsible for reporting his girlfriend as a missing person to the police and, in doing so, had disrespected him as it had brought the dreaded police to his address. To say Trevor was not very happy about being "dissed" (disrespected) would be putting it mildly, so to pay him back, he felt the victim had to be made aware of his wrongdoing. With that in mind, he went up to the victim's address with a few of his family, laid the blade tip of a large lock knife against his neck, and told him that next time he phoned the police, he would cut his throat.

Now satisfied that he had paid back in full the "diss" that he had suffered, he left threatening the victim of further repercussions if he told the police. To his credit, and despite being scared, the victim did indeed report it to the police, and now yours truly was there to deal with it. Now you may call me old fashioned, but the allegation, in my view, amounted to making "threats to kill" - clearly an offence that carried a power of arrest. So, once I had positively confirmed that Trevor was indeed the suspect, he was going to be yesterday's cold potato. To do this, I needed him to be identified, so I placed the victim in the back of my van and drove around the local streets looking for the suspect—a so-called street identification. Sure enough, as we passed a group of youths standing outside Trevor's house in Marcia

Road, my victim identified Trevor and three others as the ones present when Trevor threatened to kill him. Identification complete, I dropped the victim off and collecting a few like-minded colleagues; I drove straight to Marcia Road, where I pulled up in the middle of the road, got out and arrested Trevor and his friends.

That's when the fun started because Trevor came from a large family, and literally, the whole house mum, dad, brothers, sisters, the misper, Uncle Tom Cobbly, and all came out into the street. Where they had been in the house when I had had a cursory look only God knows, but now, all of a sudden, a veritable army had descended and a free for all kicked off that fizzled out after a minute or so when the cavalry started to arrive. End result: five detained in the back of the van, four arrests for threats to kill, and for good measure, the missing girl was taken to the station as a place of safety. Amid the shouts of derision from those we had left behind, I drove the station van back to the sanctuary at Tower Bridge Police Station, where my cargo was unloaded and rolled into the charge room. So, a good shift, really. Apart from having to write up a crime sheet and arrest notes, I had solved the whereabouts of a missing 14-year-old girl (now back with her parents), leaving prisoners detained in the cells overnight for an interview the next day by CID officers. Job done.

No problems to worry about until a day or so later when I was summoned to Southwark Police Station to see the Chief Superintendent (a position one rank or so down from God). The Southwark Chief Superintendent was the division's top police office affectionately known by the nickname "Clint" after Clint Eastwood. I was shown into Clint's office, where he was sitting behind his desk with a brown folder open in front of him. Very formally, he said, "PC Glenister, I have here in front of me a complaint regarding your actions in Marcia Road. Trevor's mother alleges you unlawfully searched her address in Marcia Road and falsely arrested her sons. Tell me about it."

Clint already knew what had happened, but to humour him, I went over the events that led up to the arrests.

Clint said, "So you did search the house then?"

I said, "Not really a search. I was invited in by Trevor, cursorily stuck my head in each room and then promptly walked back out."

Clint went on: "Well, that is a search, and as such, you should have made an entry to that effect in Book 101 (Now the Premsearch register). For not doing that, I'm giving you a caution: don't do it again. Okay?" Clint continued, "By the way, a good bit of police work; keep up the good work. I'll send a letter to the complainant notifying her that the matter has been dealt with." And with that, I was sent away.

Little did I know that this matter had brought me to Clint's notice and would be repaid in full a few months later when a new divisional crime squad was to be set up and I would be asked to join it. Joining the crime squad was a precursor to never again putting a uniform on for the remainder of my service.

Another lesson learnt: Paperwork. Don't overlook the obvious.

---ooo0ooo---

Chapter 43

The Instant Response Unit

The Special Patrol Group (SPG) bore the brunt of the public's criticism of police following the Southall Riots and the death of Blair Peach. It's strange that the media can twist things so that the good guys end up being the bad guys. It was as if the demonstrators were not responsible for throwing the bottles, other odds and ends, as well as firebombing our coach. The news coverage that day seemed to skip over the complete breakdown of law and order that we the police struggled to maintain, and focused on the death of Blair Peach, holding the police solely responsible for his death.

Prior to Southall, SPG officers were held up as the personification of what a professional police officer sought to achieve. The coveted "blue cobra" tie was something I wanted to achieve – it would be a collector's item now. Back then, Divisional Chief Superintendents fought to have them attached to their stations as their mere presence helped reduce crime figures across the board. The Southall riot changed all that as senior officers it seemed rushed to disassociate themselves en mass from any practical association with them. Overnight, the SPG had become pariahs, and just like the dinosaurs before them, had outlived their usefulness and were about to become extinct, as the SPG became the police force's sacrificial lambs.

Into the vacuum this created came the Divisional Instant Response Unit made up of a sergeant and ten relief officers from the division. Divisions found it difficult to man up these units with relief officers, so officers on weekly leave were offered overtime at enhanced rates. It is often said that one man's loss is another man's gain, and so it was for me. It provided an overtime revenue stream to tap into to earn extra money to pay the monthly mortgage, endowment and loans. It was certainly not the case that "This time next year I'll be a millionaire," but it gave me a lot more Wonga to enjoy myself with.

So, it was that on one of my rest days, I was in a carrier supervised by a Carter Street PS (who I shall refer to as M). The police, like all organisations, have their share of personnel who are a bit lightweight when it comes to working for a living. Within the uniform ranks, these operatives are known by the acronym of "FLUBa" or to give it its full title, "F-----g Lazy Useless Ba------." It was fair to say that M was universally known as being a "FLUBa." Our carrier was made up of officers from across "M." Division, and as such, each paraded at their respective stations, where they were collected in turn by the designated driver, who on this occasion was Allan. Allan was someone I had worked with before. I knew he had a way of working not that dissimilar to mine. I had met Allan prior to going to the DPG when he and I had stood guard in a ward at Guys Hospital over a prisoner whose life was apparently seriously at risk.

At that time, Allan was the authorised shot carrying a Model 10 Smith and Wesson handgun with whom I had been posted. In the event of an attack, Allan's intention was to fight them off single-handed with his pistol, a bit like the shootout at the O.K. Corral leaving them all dead or injured on the ward floor, whilst my role was pretty much to be that of a sacrificial lamb expected to distract them long enough for Allan to do the dastardly deed. That's where our in-depth planning came into its own – my distraction technique was going to be to fall to the floor on my hands and knees, and a bit like John Belushi in the Blues Brothers plead with the bad guys not to shoot me. Hopefully, that would make them either fall about laughing or stop them long enough for Allan to draw and take them out - certainly not fool proof, but better than nothing. Luckily, I never had to audition for an equity card as the bad guys never showed up.

Even when being paid overtime, it can still be a bore when all you are doing is driving around the ground basically sightseeing for eight hours, so the whole carrier, with the exception of "M," wanted to do some proactive stuff. As "M" the sergeant was in charge he kept frustrating us at every turn by saying, "Don't stop this or "Don't stop that" every time something worthwhile came onto the radar.

In fact, "M" never came to life at all until the witching hour approached as he directed the carrier towards his car parked near Carter Street so that bang on time he could jump straight into his car and be home before the last officer had been dropped off at his respective station. "M" was selfish; you bet he was. Our tour would have been the most boring one to date had fate not chosen to intervene.

As directed, Allan drove along the Walworth Road towards Carter Street Police Station when three youths appeared directly in front of us carrying a station wall clock and several other items. There they were, square in our headlights, crossing the Walworth Road towards Arnside Street, literally within spitting distance of Carter Street Police Station when the green transit van we were in stopped and out jumped a pack of police officers chomping at the bit for some action. Grabbing all three in quick succession, we separated them up so they couldn't hear what each other was saying and started to question them. Now you may think we were being picky, but it sure was strange to find three people carrying a station clock and bottles of spirit in the street at 1 a.m. in the morning, and explanations were needed pretty damned quick. All of us felt that way except "M." Clearly not impressed with this turn of events, he came over to me and said, "Let me make it clear. We are not arresting them; we will sort it out here."

I said, "You'd better speak to Allan then."

Apart from the fact that telling me not to arrest someone isn't a lawful order, it was akin to waving a red rag at a bull. A challenge that FLUBa was destined to lose. This was because as soon as he went away, I arrested my prisoner on suspicion of burglary, cuffed him and stuck him in our vehicle. Now by the time "M" got over to Allan, his plan of dealing with them in the street was not an option, and so it was that all three joined us with their goodies in the van and off to Carter Street police station charge room we went. "M" was not a happy bunny changing fifty shades of pink in as many seconds, particularly as we had arrived in a Carter Street charge room that was exceptionally busy with other prisoners. That's when the duty officer came into the equation and directed "M" to sheet our three prisoners, including all the property we had recovered. "M" was not going to have a quick off tonight, and as this was a matter for the early turn CID to deal with, all we had to do was complete our notes, make statements and go home, which is exactly what we did leaving "M" to book in the prisoners.

Who was it that said "God works in mysterious ways."? Those from other stations all jumped back into the carrier and shot off like a rocket dropping officers off along the route whilst all the time laughing like a drain at how "FLUBa" got his just desserts, perhaps learning the hard way that being selfish and lazy doesn't always work in your favour.

As for the prisoners, the Carter Street Burglary squad dealt with them the next day, where all three of them admitted committing a burglary at a working men's club and were just on their way home to have a good drink and check out their booty when we made their day. All three were charged and sent to court. I guess they pleaded guilty as apart from being told what they had done, I never heard any more about these three again.

On another occasion working as a crew member on instant response unit duties, a call came over the radio from the information room about a police response intruder panic alarm that had just been activated at a rather large house in Dulwich. Since we were in the nearby vicinity, we responded. It wasn't difficult to locate the house as we could hear the alarm prior to our arrival. Now outside the house, we immediately went about searching, securing the area and checking for signs of entry and potential suspects. Sure enough, we checked a side gate and found it held on a latch only, so we opened it and blundered along the side of the building and straight onto a patio area with a lounge door wide open. Looking further into the large rear garden, we could see perhaps three or four hundred yards away from us a lady happily gardening, accompanied by two rather large Doberman dogs.

That's when they turned and saw us on the patio, took immediate offence and started to run towards us to basically sort us out. Now, if I have to fight with a dog, I will, but since discretion is the better part of valour, I chose discretion. Quick as a flash as a unit, we ran from the patio straight through the lounge door, which we just managed to shut before both dogs slammed into it. With two dogs outside snarling away and looking like they wanted to take a few mementoes from us, we remained safe within the lounge, waiting for the gardening lady to appear, which thankfully she did. That's when she shouted something like "Nero, Brutus, come here." Thankfully both dogs obediently complied with her request, trotting off towards her and sitting down on either side of her with eyes firmly fixed on us. With the alarm still operating, ten supposedly fearless police officers sheepishly made their way out of the lounge, crossed over the patio, passing two dogs whose eyes mirrored our every move back through the side door we had entered, got back in our carrier, and drove off.

What triggered the alarm has been long lost in the passage of time, but it was not one of our finest hours and certainly not something to shout about, seen off by two dogs that had attitude. C'est la Vie

---ooo0ooo---

Chapter 44

Olympian – Not Likely

One early turn, I started out from the station at 7:00 a.m. as operator of Mike 2 that for a change was being driven by Peter. Nothing of interest came over the main set radio, and after a couple of hours of fruitless searching, we made our way to answer the call of nature at Rotherhithe Police Station. This type of call is not one that is sent via any radio set. As we were driving along Rotherhithe New Road towards the Surrey Docks one way system, two youngsters walked out of the Silwood Estate flats, clearly saw us, and with no more ado were off like long dogs back the way they had come. Not sure what they had done, I was out of the car and hot-footing it after them giving a running commentary as I went. Peter, in turn, drove off to try and get in front of them before they vanished into the labyrinth of estate alleyways.

At that time, I was in training to run the London Marathon, and although these two whippets were a good 30 yards or so ahead of me, I pegged them right back. Luckily for me, they had both stayed together, and it was a foregone conclusion that I would catch them as was the case after about 200 yards. It was then I was joined by Peter, who arrived in Mike 2. The reason they had run was that they had been reported as missing the day before. They weren't missing now, and we placed them in our car in order to take them to the police station where they would stay until collected by a responsible person. It was as I was putting them into the police car that a woman drove up and said to me, "That was impressive running. Do you want to run in our school relay? We might win it then." And with a smile, she drove off. At the station, we booked them in; job done!

After our refreshment break, we went on patrol again. It was not until 1:00 p.m. that the main set sprang to life, and we took a call to a male suspect acting suspiciously in flats off Deverell Street. The suspect's description and clothing had been provided, but as usual, the informant was anonymous, and therefore, not able to provide any other assistance.

Calls to suspects acting suspiciously are two a penny invariably the area is searched, and no trace of a suspect is found. So, we were not too hopeful that we would find our suspect this time. Arriving in Deverell Street, we parked up nearby and using shanks pony, we slipped quietly through the estate, managing to find our suspect, who was about 20 yards directly in front of us, bending down trying to get into a vehicle. Totally unaware that a posse was about to strike, Chummy carried on with his task of trying to steal a vehicle. He was like a hare trapped in spotlights when he saw us, deciding that this was not the time to test his legs. He remained where he was, dropping keys, tools and wire cutters onto the floor as we grabbed hold of Chummy and arrested him for attempted theft of a vehicle and going equipped to steal. Another lottery winner this time winning a stay at the award-winning five-star Southwark Police Hotel. Going equipped was a CID matter to investigate, so we completed our paperwork and left Chummy binned up for the late turn CID to play with. Lovely Jubbly!

I would not want you to think that we won all the time. One person who won but lost financially was Stanley. Stanley had been stopped driving a Rolls Royce in Marlborough Grove that he said belonged to a friend. When questioned, Stanley could not prove who he was, had no documentation of any type on him and couldn't say who his friend was. In addition, he had been drinking, although he was not drunk. Now Stanley was a well-built man who was not too impressed when asked to take a breathalyser and so refused, and he was arrested. The station van arrived, and that's when Stanley decided he did not want to go to the police station. Mind made up, Stanley promptly tensed his muscles and made it extremely difficult to get him into the station van. It would be fair to say that Stanley wasn't being violent, just not cooperative.

Eventually, Stanley was squeezed into the van and taken to Tower Bridge charge room, where he vented his spleen on a sergeant with a German-sounding name. Unfortunately, this sergeant was another FLUBA and allowed Stanley to partially inflate a breathalyser bag which he accepted as a negative breath test, after which he promptly left the charge room to take his refreshments. In truth, it should have been a refused breathalyser, but that's life. Another sergeant came in, and Stanley was released without charge. However, as he couldn't prove ownership of the Rolls Royce, we were obliged to keep it until he could prove to the contrary.

Stanley was shown out of the station to the front counter, where he started shouting the odds, banging on the counter and threatening everyone. Stanley had gone too far, so he was arrested for violent behaviour in a police station, taken back into the charge room, charged, and kept in custody to appear before the magistrates the next day. Stanley was convicted and fined £10. He was not happy about that, so he appealed to the Crown Court, where his case was reheard. The judge allowed the appeal stating, "Stanley was being disorderly although fell short of being violent." Stanley got his £10 back but had to pay £100 towards the court costs. A pyrrhic victory if ever there was. Stanley had spent a night in the cells, and attended two court dates, that eventually led to him being found not guilty yet still ended up being £100 out of pocket. It just goes to show that you can win, but in the game of life, still lose. C'est la Vie

---ooo0ooo---

Chapter 45

The Addams Family

So, there I was basking in the glory of a confirmed athlete when two weeks later, on a Sunday late turn, it all went head over apex. On this occasion, I was driving the station van with a female officer posted as my front seat gunner. After checking the van out, I followed the Southwark wireless car Mike 1 out of the station yard. Mike 1 turned left towards Tower Bridge Road whilst I was waiting at the gate entrance to turn right towards Rotherhithe. Timing, they say, is everything, and so it was on this occasion because turning left from Tower Bridge Road into Queen Elizabeth Street was a beige Honda with two white males. They passed Mike 1 travelling the opposite way to them and crossed immediately in front of my vehicle.

As they passed me, Mike 1 called upon the personal radio "Mike Tango 2 – that looks a good stop. We'll turn into Tooley Street and back you up."

I replied, "Mike 1 – Yes, yes. We'll get behind and stop them – Jamaica Road area." And so, it was that the Honda was now lead vehicle in convoy with Mike Tango 2 immediately behind and Mike 1 as tail end Charlie. Down Jamaica Road, right into Abbey Street and left into Old Jamaica Road, which is where I pulled the vehicle over. The two occupants were brothers from North London with the surname of Addams, members of the Addams crime Family. They were both wearing jogging outfits and trainers. Clearly visible on the back seat were two crash helmets, and I blame myself for not being quicker off the mark and putting two and two together, but perhaps this was an off day.

Either way, the brothers were separated, with one placed in the back of my van under the watchful eye of the female officer whilst the other one stood on the pavement with the Mike 1 driver Zoom. Colin and I started to search the Honda, which is when Colin found a bag hidden under the driver's seat which contained two automatic firearms.

Without any warning, the brother standing on the pavement shouted the single word "Now," and with that, he ran off in one direction whilst his brother in the van pushed past the female officer and ran off in the opposite direction. I ran off in pursuit of the brother running from my van but was some distance behind and making no impact on the distance between us as he twisted and turned through the archways of the Arnold Estate flats. It wasn't long before I turned a corner, and my runner had vanished. What's more, the other brother also managed to get away.

So, now we were left crying over spilt milk, with only the car, car keys, crash helmets and firearms to satisfy our angst. I suppose we could take some consolation that we had saved someone from being the victim of a robbery or worse and had removed two firearms from circulation, but even then, without the prisoners, it was a hollow victory. The only thing left was to arrange for the exhibits to be secured and preserved for forensic examination, write up our notes and statements and hand the whole lot over to detectives from the Flying Squad. Both brothers were later dealt with for firearm-related offences.

The learning curve for me: there is always someone faster than you, so if you're not happy with someone, cuff them first and deny them the opportunity to run away.

---ooo0ooo---

Chapter 46

Fitness Training

Clearly, having lost two good collars, I was not a happy bunny. I needed to work on my fitness. I found regular gym workouts were difficult to arrange around my three split shift work patterns, as the times and quick change over left me with a dysfunctional body clock, where I would wake up at different times. Luckily a solution was about to present itself that was too good an opportunity to miss out on. "M" Division was looking at entering a contingent of officers into the annual Barking to Southend Race Walk. As part of the deal, applicants would be given leave amounting to one day a week time off work to train.

All I knew about race walking was that it was an Olympic sport, and it pretty much means you have to swing your legs one after the other in front of you as fast as possible, making sure one foot remained on the ground at any one time. What could I lose? I was being paid to train for what was basically just a walk, albeit a long walk somewhere in the region of 34 miles.

So, along with some other shirkers—sorry colleagues—I threw my hat into the ring and joined my colleagues one day a week at the Warren to train. Supervised by inspectors, we were put through our paces, although in fairness to them, they followed us around as we walked set routes out towards Pole Hill and beyond. What I thought was going to be simple was nothing of the sort. Racewalkers walk in what can only be described as an unnatural walking style that causes the hips and legs to hurt like hell. I trained for around three or four months, not just once a week with the police but also with my long-time friend Clive.

Clive was a former Cambridge Harrier, and back then, he was as fit as a fiddle. (Sadly, time has taken its toll, and with it, Clive's natural propensity for fitness has lagged. So now, like the bionic man he relies on strapping to keep his body and soul together.) The race date of 16th May 1982 arrived, and we journeyed to Barking to start the race. Typically, the weather was very hot, and I can honestly say I was not looking forward to the hard slog I was about to embark upon. Now the rules of race walking were simple:

1.It is a race

2.A gold medal went to anyone finishing the course in less than 5 ½ hours;

3.A silver medal went to anyone finishing the course in less than 6 ½ hours,

4.A bronze medal went to anyone finishing the course in less than seven hours

5.A certificate was issued for anyone who finished in less than 7 ½ hours.

6.Everyone else got zilch.

Together with the other competitors, I went to the start line, and when the race started, I stayed with the leaders for a full two or three seconds before they started pulling away, leaving me trailing in their wake. Not surprising, really, as a few competitors were part of Team GB that had competed at the Olympic games and at the international level a fair few times.

Me at the start of the Barking to Southend Race Walk in 1982. Clive is the one behind me – photograph source not known.

Quickly realising we were not going to win, Clive and I settled in for the hard slog, punching through the pain barrier as we managed to walk up a seemingly endless Bread and Cheese Hill towards our end goal.

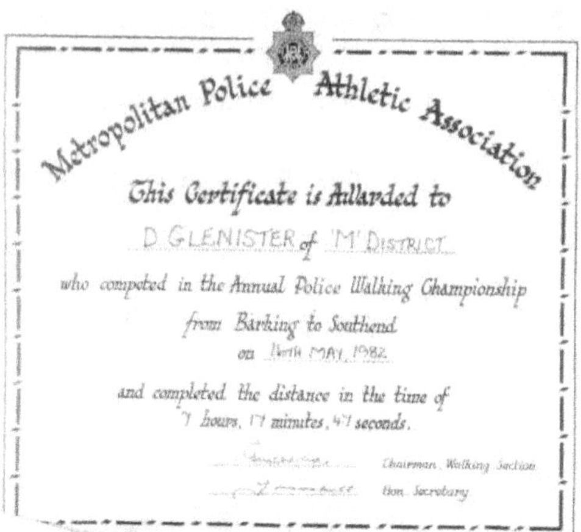

We were nowhere near the medals but we did complete the walk in just over seven hours – a duration that meant we qualified for the certificate. Better than nothing, but nowhere near the winners' winning time of around five hours.

Now exhausted, we both sat down in the shade and watched as other entrants started to finish. One poor chap was so elated at, having finished, that he did a victory jump into the air before he had passed the finishing line. Unfortunately for him, the jump had been seen by race referees who ruled that both feet were off the ground at the same time, and as such, he was disqualified. Another race entrant turned into the stadium, clearly suffering from heat-related exhaustion, so a helpful person threw a bucket of ice-cold water over him, causing his muscles to cramp up, resulting in him collapsing onto the floor in absolute agony suffering from muscle cramps.

Clive and I somehow managed to get to our feet and go in search of a well-earned drink before we cadged a lift home. Sat in a car for an hour, I arrived home and found it took 10 minutes or so just to get out of the car before I hobbled into my house where I met my not too sympathetic wife telling me what an idiot I was. Being called an idiot is something that has not changed all my married life. To say it wasn't physically demanding would be a lie. I do not know whether it was because of the physical toll this event took out of all the entrants, but it ceased completely as a race a year or so later.

Clive had enjoyed this walk so much that he decided to repay the compliment and coerced me into applying for the 1983 Gillette London Marathon. We applied and, unfortunately, were accepted as entrants. So now, we started running on a regular basis, and sure enough, I started running progressively faster, which improved my overall speed and stamina. This training came in handy when whilst off duty, I chased and caught a thief on, of all days, my birthday. There I was out with my wife Grace, meandering in and out of shops in Bexleyheath. It just so happened we went into the local Victor Values store for some food items.

I waited just inside the shop doorway by the tills whilst Grace shopped. It was while I was standing in the shop entrance that I noticed a man standing by the alcohol counter to my left, with a number of alcohol bottles that had been placed into two plastic bags sitting on the counter in front of him. It seemed to me he was in the process of purchasing the bottles of alcohol in the bags. His chosen payment method being to pay by cheque. Paying by cheque was not unusual back then, although cheques were not accepted unless supported by a cheque guarantee card, which at that time was only up to a value of £50. So different from the 'tap and pay' cards of today.

A staff member had left him alone by the counter whilst he went to the back of the shop to check the cheque and cheque card validity. As soon as the staff member was out of sight, the man picked up the two bags of alcohol from the counter and walked out of the store. I followed behind, keeping him in sight, as I was not sure what exactly was going on. That changed pretty quick when the store's assistant manager suddenly appeared on the footpath shouting words to the effect "stop thief" whereupon the man dropped the two bags and started to run off along Bexleyheath Broadway towards Welling. This was where my training came into its own. I ran after him, easily keeping pace with him as he ran along the Broadway, turning left and left again into a council car park where I saw him drop a chequebook under a car. It was shortly after he disposed of the chequebook that I caught him, placed him face-first against a wall and stuck him in a hammerlock and bar hold. Looking for assistance, I turned my head and saw Grace as my backup jogging towards me. She remained with me until other help arrived a short while later.

Ignoring my prisoner's protestations that I was hurting him, I frog marched him back through the car park and back along Broadway to the Victor Values store manager's office. The manager, a large person, was sitting in a chair at his desk. Clearly, he had just eaten a meal because in front of him was an empty plate on top of which sat a cutlery knife and fork. Now the manager's office was pretty secure with the now locked door I had just entered through being the only means of entry and exit, and with bars around the room windows there was nowhere for my prisoner to go. Since the room was secure and police were on the way, I relaxed my hold on the male.

Grace had remained with me all the time, mirroring my route back into Victor Values premises, where she now stood in the hallway immediately outside the manager's office waiting for me to re-join her.

Once I relaxed my grip, I realised I had made a big mistake because, in a flash, my prisoner pulled away from me, bent down and grabbed the cutlery knife from the plate. Now he had the knife he started turning towards me with it raised in hand, ready to use as a weapon against me. Now I have never been someone who dishes out gratuitous violence; it's just not me. However, when push comes to shove, then being nice and friendly goes out the window, and then anything goes. That's when the red mist descended, and the gloves came off. Mirroring him, I reacted fast, closed the gap between us, grabbing his raised hand with the cutlery knife with my left hand whilst using my right hand to simultaneously punch him straight in the mouth, causing it to bleed. This would have hurt him but, more importantly, distracted him sufficiently for me to take the initiative.

A short struggle followed during which my prisoner attempted to use one of his knees to impair my matrimonial prospects. Luckily, not something that he was able to carry through as I threw him to the floor, and this time restrained him in an arm lock. I believe that had I applied more pressure he would have suffered a broken arm. Chummy was clearly in pain and as such no additional increase in the force used was needed. To cut a long story short, I restrained my prisoner until the cavalry arrived, handcuffed him and took him away to the factory for processing.

The manager who up until then had been present throughout this somewhat frenetic activity performed what can only be described as a Houdini type disappearing trick by leaving the room without being seen—whereto, I don't know. As far as I was concerned, he was more useful as a chocolate teaspoon than any help to me. The whole incident in the manager's office took seconds yet seemed longer. Throughout it all, it was almost like I was on automatic pilot. Despite the red mist, I clearly saw the events unfold and could recall my actions taken to deal with the situation. What was paramount was that I had to take control and ensure the man's compliance.

Compliance is obtained through action and/or words, so I was consciously using different voice intonations to ensure there was no misunderstanding as to what my intentions were, and yet the funny thing was I couldn't remember any of the conversations that took place. Luckily, my memory was refreshed by Grace who had been outside the manager's office the whole time. The language was apparently not very complimentary or particularly politically correct—in fact, it would probably have been considered somewhat racist by today's standards. Grace took great pains to remind me of some of the words she had heard, which, to put it mildly, were of a salty nature. For the record, I do not think the man was under any illusion of what my intentions were once he became a threat to me.

The end result was that the man had used a stolen chequebook and card to purchase goods. Bexleyheath CID charged the man with a number of theft offences, for which he received a six-month prison sentence. Commander "M" called me in for a verbal commendation which back then was a rare event.

Learning curves:

1. When making an arrest, do not expect help from anyone other than those you can trust – in this instance, my soul partner – Grace, and

2. Think about what you say before saying it. You never know who might be listening.

---ooo0ooo---

Chapter 47

Jimbo

Jim Garlinge PC 488M was a thief-taker without equal. Jim, —or Jimbo, as he was called by friends and colleagues—was a police dog handler of some repute, having seen off other police dog handlers to win the coveted Black Knight trophy with his dog Inky. No small feat by any standard. Jimbo was based at Tower Bridge but, as a dog handler, had the remit to work on other divisions as needs demanded. Jimbo and Len had known each other a long time, and when not otherwise employed, Jimbo and his dog would jump into the back of the wireless car and come out on patrol with us.

A better name for Inky was Stinky. Inky would sit there next to Jimbo, looking out the window with the face of an angel, releasing silent but smelly botty burps that could and did cause us to abandon the car until it had been well ventilated. I can confirm from personal experience it wasn't just the baddies who suffered the displeasure of a police dog.

The presence of a four-legged friend available for your team is a great equaliser when you go to a disturbance where someone is hell-bent on causing carnage. Let me tell you that even potentially violent criminals think twice about mixing it when a police dog is present. Dogs are also great to have with you to take down a fleeing person. I have not heard of any runners beating a police dog in a one-to-one race. Even as a non-gambler, I might just be tempted to have a little wager that any runner would get caught.

Jimbo was a clever man who had somehow developed his own way of speaking and writing—sort of his own dialect where everyone he spoke to was "Harry," and certain words meant something specific. For example, the word "holiday" mentioned in any permutation meant someone was going to be arrested, whilst "porridge pudding" meant a prison sentence, not a dessert with his lunch.

Those who knew Jimbo learnt to understand his spoken language, but the same cannot be said for Jimbo's handwriting which was made up of arrows, lines and strange shapes not that dissimilar to Egyptian Hieroglyphics. I suspect that Jimbo would not have needed the Rosetta Stone to crack the Egyptian hieroglyphics code as it was something Jimbo pretty much used on a day-to-day basis. As such, Jimbo's arrest notes were the personification of accuracy, brevity and speed. One person he arrested for disqualified driving was brought into the station charge room. The arrest notes were written something like:

'DDTP Jam Rd – ABC123 > MD>stop A&C >MT" - and for Jimbo, that was a lot of writing.

Once the prisoner was charged, Jimbo would take his prisoner to court with his form 611 antecedents" folder suitably devoid of writing. He didn't need the folder, really, as he was able to give a person's antecedent history from memory. It was not like today, where everything has to be written down with the i's dotted and t's crossed.

Len and Jimbo worked hard and played hard, especially during the refreshment break when they would challenge numbskulls like me to a game of snooker, a deadly serious event even though it was for small stakes. Jimbo's memory was exceptional; he could even remember the exact date when Moon last bought a cup of tea, and that was no mean feat. I think Jimbo said it was in 1970, a good few years before I knew him.

That memory was tested one day as Jimbo made his way to the station because he saw a local Class A criminal driving along Jamaica Road in a Mercedes, I believe. This criminal was later charged with involvement in the Brinks Mat Heathrow Airport gold bullion robbery, for which he received a 25-year prison term.

On the day Jimbo spotted him, the car registration was consigned to his memory and committed to paper as a station intelligence report. Little did Jimbo know that this sighting would later be an important part of the Brinks Mat prosecution case and that he would be called to court as a witness. Jimbo told me later that during this trial, he felt the defence counsel was getting away with murder and was being allowed to ask outrageous questions about Jimbo's integrity – effectively saying that it was a fabrication and that he was lying. Having been called a liar, Jimbo leant his body forward into the witness box looked straight at the defence counsel, making eye to eye contact with him before saying, "But we know different, don't we?", reinforcing it with a little nod of the head. Effectively, Jimbo had turned the allegation around and, in doing so, sent a subtle message to the jury, a message that incensed the defence counsel, who now went ballistic asking Jimbo whether he was alleging that defence counsel was acting dishonest and was misleading the court.

Again, a role reversal; the defence counsel had lost the thrust of his argument and started to bluster as he had lost control. Jimbo again held eye contact with him and deliberately took his time to answer, holding the court in suspense a bit as they do on the game shows. This was court gamesmanship at its best, trying to gain an advantage with the jury, letting them take in the full impact of the drama happening before them. After a suitable time, Jimbo answered, "I wasn't talking about you, sir. I was talking about your client." You could have heard a pin drop as the courtroom went quiet waiting for defence counsel to make a suitable reply uttering those words we love to hear—'no further questions'—whereupon he slumped back down on his bench seat as Jimbo now released by the court walked out. Job done.

Jimbo joined us as a passenger in Mike 2 a fair few times, and without fail, we would make arrest after arrest. In all these arrests, one stands head and shoulders above the rest, and that arrest occurred when we were working an early turn shift. Jimbo and his dog Inky were at a loose end, so they took the opportunity to join us.

Mike 2, with a slobbering Alsatian's head sticking out a side window, went out to play.

Jimbo was in an ebullient mood, having just found out that a fingerprint identification had come back on a suspect for an aggravated burglary on an old age pensioner. The suspect was a local burglar called Philip. Philip came from a large family who were all into some type of skullduggery or other—a bit like Fagin's crew in Oliver Twist. This time though, the crime was one of the spates of burglaries in the Tower Bridge and Rotherhithe area where the victims—all pensioners—had been tied up and subjected to physical assault, each assault progressively getting more violent than the preceding one. In short, he had to be stopped, and now that his identity was known, he just needed to be found.

Whilst Philip was at large, the old and vulnerable were all at considerable risk. Despite this risk, a Detective

Sergeant (DS) had apparently sat on the fingerprint identification for a few days so that he could arrange for the suspect to be arrested before his allocated rest day. Played right, he would have had his rest day cancelled without notice earning copious amounts of money in the process. Money, it seemed, came before our duty of care to prevent another attack from happening. Jimbo was none too impressed by this, and with that, Philip became public enemy Number 1.

The plan to find and arrest him was simple; we were going to rattle a few cages, and that's exactly what we did: knocking on his parents', brothers', sisters', cousins', in-laws', and Uncle Tom Cobbly's doors. We paid them all a visit with the threat of repeat visits if they had not come back to us with information. In short, we made ourselves a pain in the backside. It took us a few hours of cage-rattling, but our efforts paid off. Our target Philip was staying at a friend's address in Lucey Way just off St. James Road that we visited a short while later. Philip didn't feel much like running away when he saw us coming along the balcony, probably due to the fact Jimbo was holding a snarling dog on a short leash, looking for any reason to let it off and do what it was trained to do.

Philip was arrested and taken to Tower Bridge police station. Once there, Philip was sheeted, and we wrote up our notes and statements. Then we left Philip and our notes with the station CID for them to deal with. As far as Jimbo's notes went, he wrote a veritable story—well at least twelve letters— "DDTP M2 - LW – P – A&C," and then, it was off to play the mandatory round of snooker and fleece some poor unwitting sap—yep – me again for tea money – job done.

Once the investigating DS was informed of Philips's arrest, he was not a happy bunny; in fact, he was hopping mad as it had scuppered his meticulous planning and forced him to get his finger out and do his job; ergo, protect the public and investigate the offences. Philip was later charged with multiple counts of aggravated burglary, for which I believe he was sentenced to an eight-year stretch in prison.

Learning curve: don't put off to tomorrow what you can do today.

---ooo0ooo---

Chapter 48

Suspicious Behaviour

My neighbours knew what I did for a living, and as such, it was no great surprise that late one evening, as I was walking back from the park with my dog Max, a neighbour stopped me in the street and informed me about two youths acting suspiciously in a neighbour's garden. Now, Max was a rather large two-year-old Rottweiler who looked more like a giant teddy bear than a lean, mean killing machine. There was every chance he had the potential to lick a person to death, but to attack someone to protect me, I had grave misgivings.

Having been on the end of two dog attacks in the last six months, Max had difficulty looking after himself, let alone me. The first dog that attacked Max was one of the largest Dobermans I had ever seen in my life, whilst the second one was an average size Alsatian. On both occasions, I was the one who jumped in and protected Max from serious injury. Seeing my dog being viciously attacked by the Doberman made my blood boil, and with the red mist taking over, I went into automaton mode. All reasoning went out the window as I stepped between the two warring parties. The Doberman's owner was present mincing around saying something like "down boy," "naughty dog," and similar nonsense.

Action speaks louder than words, so I stepped in between them and delivered a kick to the dog's solar plexus with such force that my trusty size-nine boot disappeared into its abdomen up to the sixth lace hole. It went in so far that I thought I might have killed it as the Doberman instantly lost the will to fight and pretty much keeled over on the ground whimpering. The Doberman's owner was not too impressed, but with the red mist now well and truly up, he decided discretion was the better part of valour and said not a dicky bird. I walked off with Max, leaving the Doberman where it fell. The second time Max was attacked was when he was on a leash walking alongside me on the pavement as we made our way home from the park. The garden gate and front door of a neighbour's house were open, and as we walked past, their Alsatian dog ran straight out and tried to bite max in the neck area. What the Alsatian did not know was that it had made a big, big mistake.

As with the Doberman, I put a bit of welly into a well-delivered kick, the first one made it think, and the second one sent it right over a three-foot wall back into its own front garden. Surprisingly it had lost interest in biting Max, so we continued walking along the pavement, leaving the dog with its owners. They were not impressed, but as with the Doberman, they were at fault for not controlling their dog. As we walked away, Max turned and gave a few woofs and growls like a big "Macho" dog—big of him, really, as there was no longer any threat.

So, it was with Max the liability in tow, and now held securely on a lead I went in search of the two youths. Surprisingly, I came across them a short distance away, huddling in a shop doorway. Now, luckily for me, they never knew that Max wasn't a threat to them, but provided they believed he was, their compliance was pretty much guaranteed. With my warrant card on display, I said, "Police officer! Stand against the glass and keep your hands away from your pockets. If either of you makes any sudden move, I will let the dog go, and you will both be in serious trouble." I'm glad they never noticed his stumpy little tail waggling about behind my back as I was standing talking to them. I continued, "I have been told you were in someone's garden acting suspiciously by a ground floor window; what were you doing there?" One of them said, "Looking for a place to sleep." Not satisfied, I searched them both, and on one, I found a flick knife with a five or six-inch blade. Flick knives are an offensive weapon per se, and so I arrested them both on suspicion of attempted burglary and also for possession of an offensive weapon.

The problem now was how to get them to the factory that was a fair distance away. For some reason, inspiration came to me in a flash from a program called Rawhide. It featured Gill Favour as the cattle drive master who would say, "Head them up and move them out," and so, like a cowboy, I drove them through the streets safely, twisting this way and that until finally corralling them in the police station yard and driving them in through the charge room door.

Now securely held, I told them to sit down on the charge room bench, which is when Max did his party piece. He promptly slumped onto the charge room floor, turning over on his back with his feet in the air, and tongue panting started to make a groaning noise that he kept up until I bent down and scratched his tummy. So much for my fierce dog! I think that's when they started cursing themselves for not trying to escape earlier as the realisation of Max's true nature hit them, but by then, it was too late. After I explained the circumstances of their arrests, the charge sergeant sheeted them, and, after taking their details, stuck them both in the station cells. At least now they had a place to sleep. I wrote up my notes, getting Max to put his paw mark on them just in case he was to be called as a witness and left them to the tender mercies of the station's night duty CID to deal with. I never heard what happened to them after that, but as far as my neighbours were concerned, I was the toast of the street.

For the record possessing an offensive weapon requires a person to be in a public place whilst in possession of a made, adapted, or intended weapon. The flick knife was a made offensive weapon, so my prisoner had no defence. Other items such as bottles, snooker cues and hammers are not necessarily offensive weapons unless they have been adapted or intended for use as such.

As an example of this, Len and I attended a disturbance involving neighbours. One of the neighbours by the name of Paul was a loud-mouthed rude individual who had had a few drinks and was behaving in a completely unacceptable manner. He stood in his doorway, giving it the big "I am" whilst hurling insults at his next-door neighbours. Being drunk in your own premises is not an offence; if it were, then pretty much every person in the UK would, at some time, have been guilty of that. There was an option of arresting him for causing a breach of the peace, but that would only get him a bind over and not really address the problem.

Whilst pontificating on what to do, Paul decided the matter for us as he walked from his flat out onto the balcony, literally inches into the communal area holding a glass bottle in a threatening manner. In the space of that few inches, the bottle had changed from an innocent article to an offensive weapon. That when Paul became fair game and in the words of Dirty Harry, he 'made our day" as we arrested him post-haste so fast; in fact, his feet never touched the ground as we descended the stairs and slung him into the back of the station van.

No longer so bolshie as we ignominiously drove him back to the station, where after charge, we banged him up for the night. Not surprisingly, Paul pleaded not guilty and was released on conditional bail—those conditions being that he found somewhere else to live and was not allowed to go back to within a certain distance of the address where he had been arrested except when accompanied by a police officer and then only to get his possessions. These conditions would remain in force until varied by the court, and with the earliest court date some months away, Paul was no longer around to cause trouble with his neighbours. Job done.

Whilst Paul was on bail, he was arrested for an unrelated arson matter, and since he had committed an offence whilst on bail, the court decided to keep him in custody until his court dates. Now appearing at the Central Criminal Court, Paul was sentenced to four years in prison. Now a serving prisoner, the court decided. It was not now in the public interest to pursue the offensive weapon charge, so that matter was left to lie on file. It just shows there is more than one way to skin a cat.

It was towards the end of my time on the relief that one night Len and I were driving home from the late turn. We drove into Okehampton Crescent from Upper Wickham Lane and to our right saw two lads trying to break into a parked stationary unattended bus. Stopping nearby, we walked over towards them, Len grabbed one before he could have it on his dancers, but the other one was off like a long dog, running along Okehampton Crescent before turning left into Upper Wickham Lane towards Welling and then quickly turning left again into St. Michaels Church car park.

I was a fit boy back then, and my fitness clearly started to tell as I made ground on him. He started running around and around a car, and as he did so, I said, "You know I'm going to catch you, so you might as well stop running now." To my surprise, that's exactly what he did, and so I took him into custody and walked him back to join Len at the bus. I am not sure how police were called—this was in the days before we had mobile phones—but police turned up, and we went to Belvedere Police Station, where we both earned a good few hours' overtime dealing with them.

Both were charged with vehicle interference, and in the fullness of time, we gave evidence at a not guilty Magistrates Court hearing. The end result turned out to be a draw—one was found guilty, and the other was found not guilty. You win some; you lose some. That's life. Either way, job done, and we moved on.

---ooo0ooo---

Chapter 49

Armed Response

Prior to the creation of the armed response units, central London Security was the shared responsibility of both the Diplomatic Protection Group via Ranger 500 on the one hand and the Special Patrol Group (SPG) on the other. In the wake of the Southall riots, although the SPG still performed this task, their days were numbered. That said, with the IRA mainland campaign being more aggressively wages, reducing the armed central London Security was not an option. A solution was made for divisions to mount their own 24-hour armed response capability. That's when the "80" call sign was born. The "M" Division armed response unit was allocated the phonetic call sign of "Mike eight zero." At least one of the Mike eight zero crew had to be authorised armed to the hilt with a Smith & Wesson Model 10 handgun, with six shots in the drum and six shots in the speed loader, whilst the other member was best described as being cannon fodder.

So, assuming we were unlucky enough to cross the path of a terrorist armed to the teeth with guns of all sizes, our job was to keep them pinned down until backup arrived. Let's just say that the backup would need to arrive pretty damned quick because 12 shots could be discharged in no time at all, after which the authorised shot would be left with nothing but a pistol to throw and he would become cannon fodder like his colleague. Perhaps we were both cannon fodder then.

I had still retained my authorised shot status from my time on the DPG, so I won the booby prize to undertake this role—effectively booking out a gun and driving endlessly around and around all day. I did my best to keep alert, but that is difficult when you feel you have been ordered not to respond to incidents other than those involving firearms, mind boringly numbing, to say the least, and it felt like I was doing the square route of nothing.

The only thing out of the ordinary that occurred during my watch involved an off-duty police officer letting off an imitation pistol at Sydenham Section House, where I had gone to take my refreshments in the canteen. Being armed meant you had to take refreshments at a police establishment, so, on this occasion, I chose to eat at Sydenham Section House. Parking up in the section house car park, I entered the section house, which is where I saw an officer from my relief who was a resident in the section house. We exchanged a few words, and off he went. I never gave it another thought and went into the canteen, where it just so happened some like-minded armed officers from the SPG were also having their refreshments.

My buck and I ordered our food and sat down at a table, waiting for it to be cooked. Just as our food arrived, the canteen door swung open, and Rick (I think his name is wrongly spelt and the first letter P has been missed off) squatted down into a shooting position and proceeded to fire off six shots in quick succession from a blank firing pistol similar to the Smith & Wesson handgun I was wearing. Once discharged, the door closed, and Rick legged it back to his room. To put it mildly, whilst I was not impressed, the SPG boys were livid. It was a particularly stupid thing to do. All of us could justifiably have returned fire, and our fire would have been the real McCoy.

Clearly, Rick had overstepped the mark, and it led to him being disciplined for his act of stupidity. Strange how things turn out, though – Once the disciplinary proceedings were initiated against Rick, who should accompany him and offer support throughout none other than Len the Tower Bridge Federation Rep.

I would probably have been consigned to drive continuously around and around the London Borough of Southwark armed with a gun had it not been for a crime epidemic on Southwark division that led to an invitation to join the Southwark crime squad. Eureka—it was like manna from heaven—I jumped at the chance to work in plain clothes. Little did I know that I would never again wear the blue serge uniform of a police officer for the remainder of my police service.

So, looking back on my learning years, I had managed to survive disagreements with two senior police officers on matters of law, been hospitalised with a serious eye injury, had experienced a variety of everyday police work and been awarded a Deputy Assistant Commissioner (DAC), a Crown Court and a Commander's commendation, oh and a complaint. But above all, I had enjoyed every minute of it. Long may it continue…now for the crime squad!

---ooo0ooo---